HARRIS TWEED

BY THE SAME AUTHOR
Harris and Lewis

The village of Plocropol, Harris, a typical coastal crofting community.

HARRIS TWEED

The Story of a Hebridean Industry

by

FRANCIS THOMPSON

DAVID & CHARLES : NEWTON ABBOT

7153 4319 X

Printed in Great Britain by
Clarke Doble & Brendon Ltd Plymouth
for David & Charles (Publishers) Ltd
South Devon House Railway Station
Newton Abbot Devon

Contents

List of Illustrations

7

List of Illustrations

List of Illustrations

Author's Note

This book is the result of a first attempt to gather between two covers the material for the story of Harris Tweed, or *clo mor*. Many early references to the cloth have not adequately distinguished between 'heavy coloured cloth', which could have been *clo mor*, and a cloth just as heavy, and with as many colours, which was really tartan. So far as possible, old references to coloured cloth have been assessed on an 'in-context' basis; those which were possibly tartan have been excluded, though the benefit of the doubt has been given to some. Considering the ubiquity of cloth-making in the Highlands and Islands, it is surprising to find that the many observers of the early scene failed to record full technical details of the equipment and processes used. However, the author hopes that the information presented herein on general grounds will be acceptable both to the lay and the professional reader.

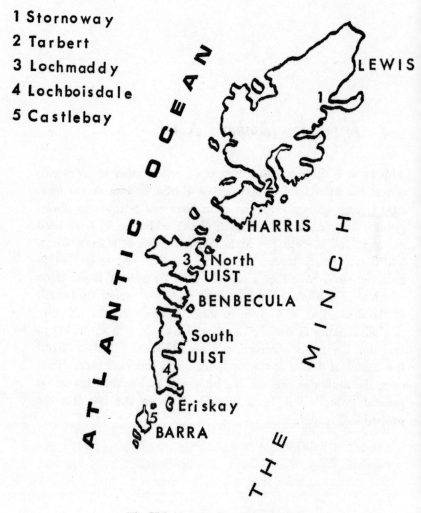

1 Stornoway
2 Tarbert
3 Lochmaddy
4 Lochboisdale
5 Castlebay

LEWIS

ATLANTIC OCEAN

1

2

HARRIS

3 North
UIST

BENBECULA

South
UIST

4

Eriskay

5
BARRA

THE MINCH

The Hebrides, showing main centres

1 Introduction

THE Hebridean contribution to the woollen-cloth manufacturing section of Scottish industry has significance for
the Scottish economy. But for that part of the Hebrides
in which the cloth known as Harris Tweed is made, the combina-
tion-island of Lewis-with-Harris, it is the economic basis of
existence. The extreme geographical concentration of the manufacturing elements, and the fact that Harris Tweed is woven by
self-employed weavers using foot-operated treadle looms, makes
the whole industry remarkable.

The total area of the Outer Hebrides, of which Lewis-with-
Harris forms the largest part, is about 716,000 acres, with a
population of some 34,000. The Outer Hebrides form a long
chain of islands from the Butt of Lewis to Barra Head—a wall
nearly 130 miles long serving as an effective shield for the north-
western part of the Scottish mainland against the buffeting of
the Atlantic Ocean. The islands are separated from the mainland
by the Minch, a broad and restless channel varying from 30 to
40 miles wide. This linear pattern of islands for centuries attracted
many kinds of people: some for political, some for economic
reasons, and some have been mesmerised by that indefinable
'Celtic twilight'. This latter 'romantic' aspect has been somewhat

13

enhanced by the fact that the islands once supported a population and way of life lagging far behind anything considered an acceptable degree of civilisation in other parts of Europe.

Lewis is in the county of Ross & Cromarty and has four parishes: Barvas, Uig, Lochs, and Stornoway. Harris, with the other islands of the Outer Hebrides, is in the county of Inverness-shire, and has only one parish. The only town of considerable size is Stornoway, with a population of over 5,000, which acts as an island port and seat of administration for Lewis. Harris has the much smaller capital village-centre of Tarbert with a population of some 400. Tarbert has a direct sea connection with Skye and the southern isles, and by road with Stornoway.

The Hebrides are composed almost wholly of archean gneiss. This hard and ancient rock, called by Geikie the geologist the oldest known fragment of Europe, reaches a height of 2,622 feet in the Clisham, the high hill on the boundary of Harris and Lewis; several peaks in this area reach some 2,000 feet. Only on the lower slopes can anything like vegetation survive, and then it clings for dear life to scraps and whiffs of poor earth collected in crevices and cracks. The gneiss supports vast plateaux of rolling moors which are broken up by hundreds of freshwater lochs abounding with trout. Natural drainage is provided by small, fast-flowing rivers well known for their salmon and fully one-quarter of the Lewis-with-Harris island area of 528,165 acres is water. This fact makes the island difficult to traverse and some parts are almost inaccessible unless one undertakes a long but not uninteresting journey on foot over the moors. These moors are peat: 15 ft deep in places, it is judged by experts to be the accumulation of the last seven thousand years or so. The megalithic circle at Callanish, Lewis, reckoned second only to Stonehenge, was erected c 1800 BC. When Sir James Matheson, proprietor of Lewis during the last century, had the stones excavated in 1857-8, they were almost covered by peat. A depth of 5 ft was removed from the site, leaving the stones much as they are now, prominent sentinels on their hill site overlooking Loch Roag.

14

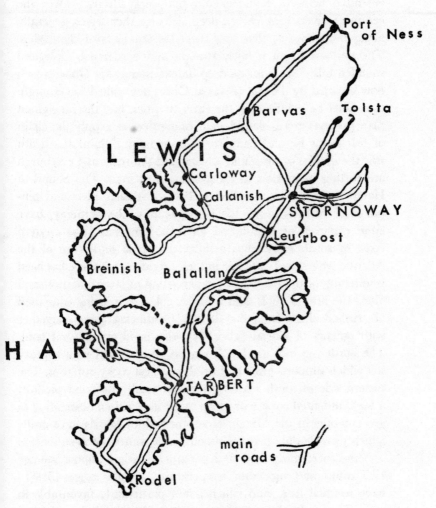

Lewis and Harris, showing main roads

Introduction

Harris is an extremely rugged land; geographically it is an island complex. In the north, the land is extremely barren, with extensive fields of boulders and bare-rock surfaces. Over the centuries, rivers have carved deep clefts for themselves, generally along fault lines so that they meet the sea in fiord-like gashes. The southern coast is fairly straight and bordered by low and rounded hills. There is one deep indentation at the Obbe, a loch now invaded by the sea. It was at Obbe, now called Leverburgh, that Lord Leverhulme, in the early twenties, had the far-sighted plan to develop an island-based fishing fleet to supply the chain of fish shops he had established throughout Britain. His death saw the demise of his island scheme and the relics at Leverburgh are rusting memorials to the ambitions of man. The Sound of Harris has been justly called a chaos of islands, islets and pin-points of rock. Some of the larger islands, like Berneray, have large expanses of sand-based soil called machar. The western coast of south Harris has to bear the brunt and force of the Atlantic waves, truly oceanic in their origin so that there has been a softening of the coast and the deposition of large tracts of sand along the littoral. This sand is highly calcareous, being composed of crushed shells from the shallow Continental Shelf, together with patches of glacial debris. It forms good agricultural land. The bordering hills are low, rounded and covered with a peaty soil which supports grass and heath amongst rocky outcrops. The eastern side of south Harris presents a totally different picture; a high, indented coast with steep rocky slopes often descending to great depths in the Minch. Here, the folk of Harris have crofts which provide only bare subsistence; sometimes not even that.

Altogether, rainfall (50-80 in per annum), wind (annual average 17·5 mph) and moderate temperature (annual range 15·4°F) have resulted in a land which is not particularly favourable to man. Thus, it has been to the sea that the island folk have looked for the basis of their economy, at least since the eighteenth century; but today fishing is in a parlous state with only a glimmer of hope on the horizon of its future. Crofting, as a way of life,

16

Page 17: (above) The village of Garenin, Lewis; (below) Crofts in south Harris.

Page 18 : (above) The Lewis linear village of Balallan (town of Allan); (below) Blackface sheep on the shore at Scarista, west Harris.

has much to recommend it for those who do not mind hard work with relatively little material return. In terms of economics however, even the staunchest crofter will admit that, unless he is one of the favoured few, his income from the land is far below an ample material reward. Coupled with the ancillary occupations of fishing and the weaving of Harris Tweed, however, crofting offers a good reason for staying in what, to the unseeing eye, is a most inhospitable land. In many townships in Lewis, for instance, more than half the families have a loom, and it has replaced fishing as the economic mainstay.

BLANKETS AND PLADDING

Among primitive nations cloth must have been first woven from undyed wool, or from the mixture of natural white and black, which is still common in the popular 'Shepherd's Check'. The manufacture of wool is supposed to have been introduced to the British Isles by the Belgae, who reputedly arrived in Britain about 300 BC, and woollen garments were certainly in use in the time of Julius Ceasar. As in other parts of the Highlands and Islands, coarse woollen cloth has been made in the Hebrides for centuries. Since the people were virtually self-supporting, the production of cloth was for domestic use; when, however, there was a surplus, it was sold, bartered, or used instead of money, which was often non-existent, in the payment of rents. 'Quhyte plaiding' is mentioned in a sixteenth-century document as constituting a kind of rent in Lewis and Harris. Thus the weaving industry was recognised some centuries ago as having economic significance.

That the surplus of cloth available could be considerable is shown in many old records of trade. In 1656 'pladding' was one of the items of trade brought by Highland boats to Glasgow. Much earlier, in 1335, one entry in the list of wardrobe expenses of John of Isla included 'A crimson vest of woollen cloth, one pair of tartan truis, one ditto of red cloth, three ells of yellow

B

Harris, showing main townships

woollen cloth for a hood . . .' In the year 1582 it was said of the Highlanders that: 'They delight in marled clothes, specially that have long stripes of sundry colours; they love chiefly purple and blue. Their predecessors used short mantles or plaids of divers colours, sundry waies divided; and amongst some, the custom is so observed to this day; but for the most part they are browne, more near to the colour of the hadder (heather); to the effect when they lie amongst the hadder the bright colour of their plaids shall not betray them . . .'

In 1688, William Sacheverell, Governor of the Isle of Man, visited the Western Isles. He says, 'They now generally use coat, waistcoat, and breeches, as elsewhere, and on their heads wear bonnets made of thick cloth, some blew, some black, and some gray . . .' This reference to black and grey as being common cloth colours in the seventeenth century, contrasts with the colours of cloth woven for various sections of the ancient Gaelic society. The old laws laid down that there was to be one colour in cloth woven for servants' wear; two colours in cloth for rent-paying farmers; three for officers; five for chiefs; six for *ollamhs* and poets; and seven in the clothes woven for kings and queens. The omission of cloth containing four colours is interesting; most numbers had a significance in Celtic life but not the number four.

By the middle of the nineteenth century, grey was the common colour worn by Highlanders, though it was not particularly popular. In *Lays of the Deer Forest* (1848), John Sobieski and Charles Edward Stuart mention the reason for grey being a resented colour.

That peasant colour, called in the middle ages 'hodden grey'—then the distinctive wear of 'churls' and beggars, and now of the Highlanders—was derived by the latter from the Border 'maud', or Cheviot shepherd's plaid, first introduced among the clans with the flocks of Cheviot sheep. The coming of the 'white faces' (sheep) and grey plaid is still remembered in some of the glens . . . It was called 'brat-gaill'—the foreigners' rag; and 'riochd-mallaichte'—the accursed grey. In the middle ages the hodden grey was in all countries a despicable garb, the characteristic of all that was base and ignoble, the attribute of the churl and peasant, in opposition to the green and scarlet of the gentle blood. Accordingly, in the sumptuary Acts of the Scottish Parliament, it was prescribed as the working habit of the laborious orders (14th Jac. II, 71) and thus the husbandmen and servants 'did weare coarse cloth made of grey, or skie colour'.

There was a second reason for the colour grey being disagreeable to Highlanders. To them, grey was what black was to other societies, a personification of the sombre, of the superstitious, and of death, and hence was associated with the half-world of ghosts and spirits with which the Celtic temperament kept an uneasy alliance.

McIan, in his *Highlanders at Home* (1900) observes:

The (Highland) shepherds wear grey plaid common in the great sheep districts on the Border counties and now so well known everywhere as a material of general use. It is not, however, of Highland origin but was first seen on the shoulders of southern farmers, who visited the north in the way of business. The MacLeods of Luskintyre asserted that the first plaid of this pattern (shepherd's check) seen in Skye was worn by Hogg, the celebrated 'Shepherd' poet; but even the gamekeepers and forresters on the estates of some Highland nobles and gentlemen are seen to the present day arrayed in dresses of this homely hue.

From about the middle of the eighteenth century, the manufacture of cloth rose to meet the demand of an increasing population. In the Highlands, spinning schools were set up and establishments on factory lines built to make the cloth, though the Islands did not participate in this industrialisation. From the

New Statistical Account of Scotland (1845) the following extracts indicate the widespread interest in cloth-making:

Inverness: In the woollen manufactury, for the weaving of coarse clothing and Highland plaids and tartan . . . The proprietor of it also has a carding-mill for the preparation and spinning of wool.

North Uist: The men dress in kelt or cloth of native manufacture; and the women are seen to most advantage in beautiful strips and tartans of their own (hand) manufacture.

Stornoway: Country clothes, called kelt, sell from 1s 6d to 4s per yard of four feet. The dress of the country people of this parish is made of kelt and plaid, their own manufacture; their coats and short clothes are made of grey and blue stuff; cotton and check shirts are worn on Sundays; but through the week, plaiden shirts, Hebridean flannel.

Lochs (in Lewis): There are many articles manufactured here, for home consumption; such as blankets for beds, coarse cloth, various in colour and quality, but chiefly striped, stockings, etc. The poor people generally rear the wool from which they manufacture their scanty store of these necessities . . . The only resident tradesmen in Lochs are boat-builders, weavers, and tailors . . . The females are accustomed to spin yarn, principally with the spindle and distaff, and also to make stockings.

Cloth-making was an important element in the economy of St Kilda. In May 1877, John McDairmid, and officer of the Highland & Islands Agricultural Society, sailed from Greenock on HMS *Flirt* with food to relieve hardship among the St Kildans. He found that the men on the island were mostly tailors, shoemakers and weavers and that every house had a loom. The islanders made all their own clothing (the men making the women's dresses) and they sold a good deal of blanketing and tweeds. In nearly every house was a spinning-wheel and a large pot in which the yarn was dyed. The women were expert

23

knitters. For tweed made on the island, 27d to 30d per yard was received; for blanketing, 28d per yard. Cloth was measured by the 'big yard' which was 49 inches. Though much of the island's export of cloth went to the Scottish mainland, a considerable quantity was sold direct to tourists who made the great adventure to see the tiny island community of St Kilda which lived seemingly on the very edge of the known world.

TWEED

The word tweed is applied to woollen suiting and coating cloths of varying degrees of roughness, from coarsest homespuns to finer, more dressy cloths. The poor conducting property of woollen-spun material, giving protection from heat and cold alike has long been noted. Not for nothing has it been considered particularly suitable for outdoor sports wear in temperate climates.

In the making or ordinary cloths there are two sets of threads: the warp, running the length of the web of cloth; and the weft (old word: woof), comprising the cross threads. In the simplest form of cloth-making, the first weft thread is passed under the first warp thread and over the second and so on right across. The second weft thread, which is really the same thread on its return journey in the opposite direction, passes over the first warp thread and under the second. This simple weave is called 'plain weave', is the foundation weave of most primitive cloths, and is typical of the Irish woollens such as Donegals.

The Scottish woollen cloth however, uses the 'tweed weave', which is not a peculiar Scottish invention but a logical development of the weaver's craft. The basis of this weave is threads which cross over two and under two, and at the same time move forward to the right or left. This construction of cloth has been known as the 'two and two twill', the 'Cassimere twill', and, in Scotland, the 'common twill'. Scotland was noted for the production of this denser, very pliable and heavier twill cloth. The word 'twill' became 'tweel' in the Scots tongue. 'And ye maun reel the tweel, John,' says Mistress Grumly in the old Scottish song, and as 'tweel' the cloth woven in the Borders of Scotland was sold to southern markets. The name may well have travelled north to describe the cloth made in the Highlands, though plaiding was more often a northern description.

In the Gaelic west, it was simply *clo* (cloth), with the adjective *mor* to describe it as the 'big cloth' on account of its heaviness and coarseness.

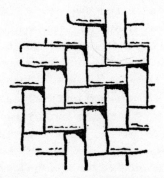

Twill or tweed, in which the threads
cross over two, under two

And so the word 'tweed' itself may well be derivative, for it required only the alteration of the letter 'l' in 'tweel' to 'd'. The association of the Borders with the River Tweed might also have been instrumental in bringing about the change of word. Whatever the real reason, the following tale is one of happy coincidence.

For years the Border shepherds had worn plaids of a black-and-white checked design. Then, about 1825, men began to use the checked cloth for wraps. The suitability of the cloth for leggings was obvious. In 1830 Archibald Craig, an Edinburgh woollen merchant, received an enquiry from London for 'a coarse woollen black and white checked stuff made in Scotland, and expected to be wanted for trouserings'. Craig sent off some cuttings from the seam of a cloak. The reply came back that it was exactly the kind of material required and an order for some half-dozen pieces of cloth arrived. In time, the Scotch tweels became well known in London and a London merchant, James Locke of Regent Street, played a large part in their promotion. About the year 1840 a quantity of tweel was invoiced by Watsons of Hawick to James Locke. The usual legible copperplate handwriting of the clerk was reduced to a scribble as this rush order was noted on an invoice. In time, James Locke read his invoice, mistood an 'l' for a 'd' and the name was born; a distinctive name for a distinctive cloth, and it has been that way ever since.

This trade in woollen cloth in the valley of the River Tweed had in fact been a staple industry of Scotland for hundreds of years. Some time after the Treaty of Union between Scotland and England in 1707 (opposed bitterly by many Scots who felt their politicians were selling their birthright for less than a mess of potage), a board was set up to encourage, among other industries, the manufacture of woollen cloth. This board improved the methods used to produce the cloth by giving instruction and by offering prizes for good work. The cloths made in the early years were heavy, well-felted fabrics, much like the strong dense cloths worn by seamen to this day. Pure virgin wool was used; mungo, shoddy and other re-manufactured wools, such as are used extensively in the West Riding of Yorkshire, were hardly recognised. The other distinctive aspect of the Border cloths was that the yarn used was spun on the woollen system, ie carded, not combed as in English worsted. The result was that the woollen goods from the Borders, and later from the other cloth-making areas of Scotland, bore a stamp of quality, and were in world demand.

In the early days of the Border woollen industry, the cloths were made chiefly for male wear. They were mostly of dark colours usually grey, in contrast to the cloths of bright colours made in the Highlands from vegetable dyes. Later, when indigo dyeing was better understood, blue cloths, known as 'Galashiels

26

Blue', were produced. The cloths were cheap and coarse and made from Cheviot wool, which was often very tarry. With the introduction of new techniques in cloth-making, cloths became lighter and suitable also for women's wear. The introduction of a range of district checks also gave an impetus to the sale of the cloth known as tweed.

The cloth which is today known as Harris Tweed has the addition of an adjective to denote its place of origin, the Outer Hebrides in general and particularly Harris. But it is much more than this, for it denotes a tweed which is handwoven, as distinct from the mill-made cloth of the Borders. From cottage-industry beginnings, the present-day stature of the Harris Tweed industry is out of all proportion to its actual size and method of manufacture. It tends to be an industry of paradoxes, in spite of which it has succeeded where other industries, with more formally-recognised methods for manufacture and commercial organisation, have often faltered and too often failed. It is also an industry whose organisers have an aim beyond that profit motive which is the *raison d'être* of commercial enterprise : they have a remarkable understanding and recognition of its social and economic value to the people of the Western Isles. In this respect the industry is unique.

2 *The Old Ways*

THE art and practice of weaving is one of man's most ancient occupations, dating from his first desire to have some means of protection against the cold and rain. Explorations of early Biblical sites have unearthed samples of cloth woven from 2,000 to 3,000 years before Christ. In Scotland, archaeological excavations have uncovered evidence that in later prehistoric times cloth-making was one of the occupations of the house or settlement. Among the ruins of the Broch of Midhowe, at Rousay in Orkney, there have been discovered weaving combs made of cetacean bone. This was a favourite material for these implements, for such combs have been discovered in brochs in many other places throughout Scotland, in Shetland, Caithness, Kircudbrightshire, Perthshire, Argyll, and in the earth-houses of the Outer Hebrides. These combs are simple in design; the teeth were scraped out by a pointed knife or other similar instrument, and seldom are they ornamented. Some combs in the National Museum of Antiquities in Edinburgh show evidence of having had their teeth sawn out by the use of very thin-bladed tools which kept the teeth straight and true.

Closely associated with the weaving comb in the manufacture of fabrics is the spinning whorl, used with the distaff in spinning

28

the wool into yarn or thread. Whorls are not often found around the ruins of brochs, caves or other early domestic settlements but occasionally they have been found, singly, around old shieling places on the moors, some distance away from the settlement. These shielings were used as summer dwellings for womenfolk

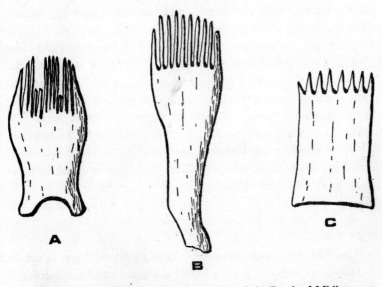

Ancient weaving combs found among the ruins of the Broch of Midhowe, at Rousay in Orkney. Made of cetacean bone. a: thirteen teeth, three broken, the sides and base of handle concave; b: ten long teeth, sides and base of handle imperfect but originally concave, 5¾ in long; c: eight short teeth, one with a broken point, base of handle swells out to a greater width than the teeth, 3½ in long

tending the cattle on the hill grazing. To use their time usefully, the women made butter and cheese, and spun wool. This task was performed in the open air, in no particular place on the hillsides, thus whorls tended to be lost and are now usually found only in isolation. One of the few exceptions to this is the vitrified fort of Finavon in Angus, where evidence points to the existence of a small textile industry, and a number of spindle-

29

whorls were found, one decorated with finely engraved lines. Another sign of cloth-making activity on excavated sites are loom-weights, often grooved for a cord to rest in.

In a manuscript of some 1,000 years ago known as the *Senchus Mor* there is mention of the implements of cloth-making: spindles, spinning-stick, the wool-bag, weaver's reed, distaff-spool stick, flyers, needles, beams, and swords (weaving sticks). Mention is also made of the *glaisin* dye. This is believed to have been a green dye and the process of making it is described so: 'The glaisin is gathered; then made into cakes; there is a first *cru*; then a second *cru*; then a third and finishing stage'. The *Senchus Mor* mentions weaving as being a highly-skilled craft with the cloth produced being extremely artistic. Women were the spinsters, weavers and dyers. The women's share of the material (if divorced) was one-eighth after shearing; one-sixth in locks; one-third when first combed, or the grease put in; and half the cloth, or the thread and cloth.

THE WOOL

The Cheviot sheep, originally known as the Long-faced or White-faced sheep, is said to have been introduced into Scotland about the year 1372. It is classed as a mountain sheep, as is the Scottish Blackface. These two breeds have for centuries provided the wool for Scottish cloth, and are said to have originally come from the north of England. Between them they ousted an earlier, if not primitive, breed of sheep called the Tan-faced. About 1760 the two breeds came under close investigation as to their respective merits and demerits as producers of mutton and wool. The Blackface fleece (weight 3-4 lb) is coarse, long (staple length 8-12 in) and open. It contains a considerable proportion of kemp or dead hairs, the result of feeding on moor mountain ground. The Cheviot fleece (weight 4-4½ lb) is much shorter and finer (staple length about 4 in) and crimpy, clean and dense; the finest is almost free from kemp.

Sir John Sinclair introduced the Cheviot to Caithness in northern Scotland in the year 1791. From there it spread rapidly into the neighbouring county of Sutherland so that Patrick Sellar, of Highland evictions fame, remarked: 'From 1805 to 1820, from a few hundred Cheviot sheep that the county then contained, their number had so increased that 100,000 fleeces were sent annually to the manufacturer'. When Sir John introduced the Cheviot to the north they had never been known by any other name than the Long- or White-faced sheep; these names had little meaning as other breeds could be so described. Sir John, in a moment of inspiration, called them Cheviots, and so they have been known ever since.

It is said that James Menzies of Culdares, the Covenanting colonel who captured the Marquis of Huntly at Dalnabo in Strathdon, introduced the Blackface sheep to the north of Scotland. The colonel, in his youth, served under Gustavus Adolphus. About 1760 he imported a flock of Lammermuir or Blackface sheep to his estate in Glenlyon, where he had some difficulty in getting the breed accepted; the women complained bitterly about the coarseness of the wool. Eventually, there was the intermixing of Blackface and Cheviot breeds now familiar in the Highlands and Islands.

WASHING

The first stage in the transformation of wool to cloth was the shearing or clipping of the wool from the sheep. This wool had then to be prepared for dyeing by scouring. Rainwater was regarded as being the most suitable medium for this; hard water was sometimes softened by adding bran. The fleece was opened out to remove any soiled portions, together with any foreign matter such as grasses, seeds, etc picked up by the wool while on the sheep's back on the hills and all natural fats and greases had to be washed out of the wool. This was extremely important. Unscoured fleece ready to be 'dyed in the wool' usually contains

31

a good deal of lanolin; yarn which has been handspun 'in the grease' before dyeing still contains either this lanolin or other oil which has been added in the carding process to facilitate the hand-spinning. In either case, however, the grease must be removed completely before dyeing, or the mordant and dye will not 'take', ie be absorbed by the fleece or yarn. The scouring water was brought slowly to hand-heat and soaps used to produce a lather. The scouring was repeated several times until a small tuft of fleece, when squeezed out, looked perfectly white. In the scouring process it was necessary to see that the fleece was moved only occasionally, as there was always the tendency to 'felt', ie for the wool fibres to matt together. After the fleece had been rinsed in successively cooler waters, it was finally removed and laid out on springy grass or heather out of direct sunlight but where a good circulating current of warm air would dry it quickly.

DYEING

Usually wool was dyed in a mass before the carding. In some areas it was spun in its natural colour and then dyed in hanks or skeins, but if not done carefully this would result in uneven colouring. It was often done where only small quantities of yarn were required for a particular purpose.

The colouring of cloth is an art almost as ancient as that of weaving itself. Julius Caesar relates that in Britain the people stained their bodies blue with woad or weld; the Bible tells of garments dyed or stained with the juices of grapes and berries, and Joseph's coat of many colours needs no comment. Analyses of mummy cloths have shown that the ancient Egyptians were familiar with the use of the metallic salts of aluminium and iron. They also used the bodies of insects known as kermes, the Mediterranean equivalent of cochineal, to make a scarlet dye for wool treated with alum. For thousands of years indigo has been used in the East, and today it is still a standard for maximum fastness to light, though now made synthetically and the method used in its application much improved. The Romans obtained the yellow dye, saffron, from crocus plants.

The preliminary stage before dyeing was mordanting. This helped to fix the dye, in other words to make it 'bite', (mordant: from French *mordre*, to bite). Some dyes did not require a mordant and were known as substantive dyes. Where it was difficult to obtain the usual chemical mordants, *fual* was used. This was urine (long kept in a special tub). The other mordants were, when available, iron (ferrous sulphate), one of the oldest of its kind and sometimes called copperas; alum (potassium aluminium sulphate), which also has a longish history as a mordant; and bichromate of potash (potassium dichromate), which is a fairly modern mordant referred to as chrome in dyer's jargon. It gives a beautiful soft feel to the wool and a range of slightly muted colours. Tin (stannous chloride) was used to give really bright shades and also as an additive to other mordants; the fir club moss was often used instead of alum. The mordant was dissolved thoroughly in hot water before it was added to the mordant bath, which held sufficient cold water to cover the fleece without compressing it, and the whole was brought slowly to the boil; then the fleece was allowed to cool down after an hour or so before rinsing in several changes of water. When alum was used, the damp fleece was stored for some days before rinsing, as this mordant took longer than others to penetrate the wool fibres. When chrome was used, the bath had to be provided with a lid to exclude the light, the fleece had to be dried in the shade and dyeing had to follow almost immediately.

In the old days the dyer's craft bordered on an art form; it was a particularly slow and uncertain process. Good dyeing was once regarded as so important that 'true' and 'false' dyeing were recognised and closely regulated by the French Governments of the eighteenth century. In Scotland, the colours used for cloth, especially the tartans, have for centuries been obtained from indigenous plants and trees. That many hundreds of these were

33

used for dyeing, throughout the Highlands and Islands, is shown by the wide variety of clan tartans.

The dyeing process was carried out in the open air, generally beside a stream of fresh, clear water—rainwater or soft peaty water being considered the best. A large black iron pot was placed over a hot peat fire, the dyeing agents were put into the boiling water, and an infusion like tea was made. The pot was kept continuously on the boil, the wool being lifted out with a long stick for examination from time to time, until thoroughly dyed. It was then removed and washed in fresh water until perfectly clean; if blue was the dye used, the washing was done in salt water to preserve the colour. The wool was laid out on heather to dry, and if in wool-fibre form it was then taken for teasing and carding before being spun into yarn. If in yarn form, it was hung out to dry, then gathered into balls or clews ready for the weaver.

The dyeing process was a skilled one and the deep knowledge of plants required was, more often than not, handed down from mother to daughter through successive generations. The colours of cloths produced throughout the Highlands and Islands tended to reflect local variations in flora.

The following are some of the sources of dyes used in the early days in the manufacture of *clo mor*.

Blue: Woad (*isatis tinctoria*, Gaelic *glas-lus* or *guirmean*). Though now extinct as a cultivated plant in Britain, it is used on the Continent. Bilberry or blaeberry (*vaccinium myrtillus*) with alum; elder (*sambucus nigra*) and broom (*cytisus scoparius*) with alum gave a pale blue.

Yellow: Dyer's rocket (*reseda luteola*, Gaelic *lus-bhuidhe mor*). This gave an excellent yellow dye; as did broom (*cytisus scoparius*, Gaelic *bealaidh*); mugwort (*artemisia vulgaris*, Gaelic *liath-lus*); saffron crocus (*crocus sativus*, Gaelic *croch*); and the crab-apple tree, ash, buckthorn, poplar, elm, bog myrtle, ash-tree root, bracken root, St John's wort, teasel, and sundew with ammonia.

Page 35 : (above) Sheep on Shielabost beach, Harris; (below) sheep-shearing in Lewis.

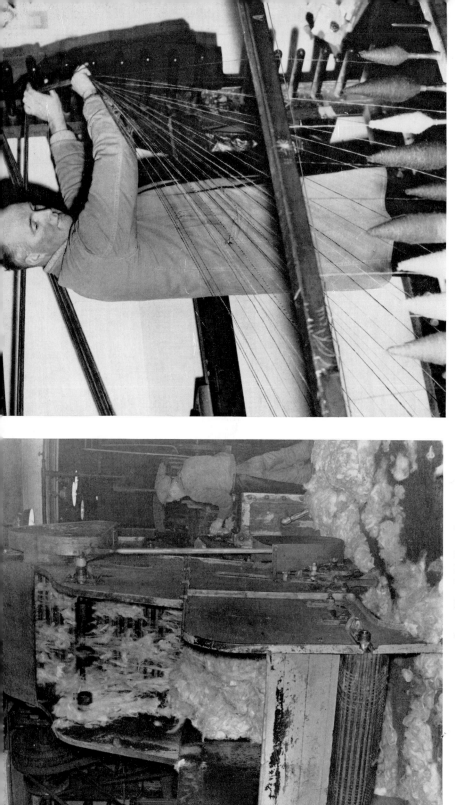

Page 36 : (left) Scouring wool in a Stornoway mill; (right) stake-warping, a mill process.

Red: Stone parmelia (*parmelia saxatalis*, Gaelic *crotal*). This plant is flat, with leaf-like indentations and round saucer-shaped protuberances on its grey-green upper surface. Its underside is black. It produced a reddish-brown dye and was a favourite shade for Harris Tweed in the early days of the industry. So much did the Highlander believe in the virtues of *crotal* that hose dyed with it was said to prevent the feet from becoming inflamed or blistered from walking long distances. At one time it was used so extensively in the Western Isles that the plant became almost extinct and supplies of it had to be obtained from Skye and the mainland. These stone lichens were so valuable a natural resource that a proverb runs : 'Better the rough stone that yields something than the smooth stone that yields nothing'. Also used for red dye was the tormentil (*tormentilla potentilla*, Gaelic *leannartach*); lady's bedstraw (*galium verum*, Gaelic *ruamh*); fir club moss (*lycopodium selago*, Gaelic *garbhag-an-t-sleibhe*); rue-root, and the madder root.

Black or Grey: Yellow flag iris (*iris pseudacorus*, Gaelic *seileasdar*); meadowsweet (*filipendula ulmaria*, Gaelic *lus-cuchulainn*), alder-tree bark (*alnus glutinosa*, Gaelic, *fearna*), root of the common dock (*rumex obtusifolius*, Gaelic *copag*), oak bark and acorns (*quercus robur*, Gaelic *darach*), and water-flag root.

Dark Green: Ling heather (*calluna vulgaris*, Gaelic *fraoch*). Was used with alum to give a dark green colour. It must be pulled before flowering and from a dark shady place. Also available from teasel (*dipsacus sylvestris*, Gaelic *am bearnan-bride*), iris leaf, broom, and whin or furze bark.

Magenta: Dandelion (*taraxacum officinale*, Gaelic *lus-an-fhucadair*).

Orange: Barberry root (*berberis vulgaris*, Gaelic *gearr-dhearcag*), peat soot (also used for a dirty yellow); bramble (*rubus fruticosis*, Gaelic *dris*).

c

37

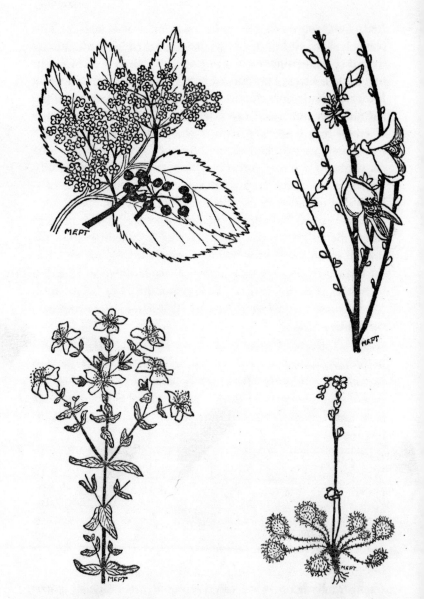

Plants used for producing dyes: (top) elder, blue; broom, yellow; (below)
St John's Wort, yellow; Sundew, yellow

Purple or Crimson: Cudbear (*lecanora tartarea*, Gaelic *corcar*). This plant was first dried in the sun, then pulverised and steeped in urine, the vessel being rendered airtight. It was left thus for three weeks then it was boiled with the yarn it was to dye. In some parts of the Highlands the people eked out their livelihood by the proceeds from the supplies of this lichen which they sent to the dyers in Glasgow.

In all the black dyes, copperas was an almost essential constituent. A really magnificent black dye was obtained by boiling the bark of the briar, oak or alder. Dr Lightfoot, an enthusiastic botanist who accompanied Thomas Pennant on the latter's second voyage to the Hebrides in 1772, says (in *Flora Scotica*, 1777) of the root of the yellow bedstraw :

The Highlanders use the roots to dye red colour. Their manner of doing so is this:- The bark is stripped of the roots, in which bark the virtue principally lies. They then boil the roots thus stripped in water, to extract what little virtue remains in them, and after taking them out, they last of all put the bark into the liquor, and boil that and the yarn they intend to dye together, adding alum to fix the colour.

CARDING

To make woollen yarn the wool was carded, that is carefully scraped between two flat hard boards covered with strong wire teeth embedded in leather and known as cards or carders. In this process, all the short and long fibres of the wool were methodically tangled and thoroughly blended into a mass of equal density throughout. In the earliest times the wool fibres had to be teased out by hand to a well-mixed mass; a long, laborious and tiring job. Cards were both left-handed and right-handed. One card was held firmly against the knee; the other card was held in the hand. The wool was placed between the opposing teeth and the to-and-fro motion of the cards loosened and softened the wool very effectively. Occasionally, three sets of cards were used: the first to tease the wool between teeth which were set widely apart; the second, with teeth set at shorter intervals, to smooth the fibres; and the third, with fine teeth set close together, to produce fine slivers or rovings. If, as was usual, the wool had been scoured and dyed before the carding process, certain amounts of oil, fats,

Hand cards

or grease were now added, usually about a fifth of the weight of wool. Fish-oil was never used; tallow, lard or the butter from ewe's milk was the lubricating agent used in the Western Isles. The fibres were thus prevented from damage or breakage.

After the wool was carded, it was placed on the flat back of one of the cards and with the aid of the other rolled into loose rods or rolls which were very smooth and light. Carding, like spinning, was a task for the long winter nights, and was usually done to the background of the *ceilidh*, at which songs were sung and tales were told of the days in Gaelic history and the still older days in Celtic mythology. The work was always done by women and girls.

SPINNING

From the carder, the wool was received by the spinner in rods or rolls, a convenient form for the well-known spinning wheel.

In earlier times, however, a more primitive method was used to spin the wool into yarn or thread. This was the spindle and whorl. The theory of spinning is simply that fibres, arranged longitudinally and then twisted, will give a long, continuous

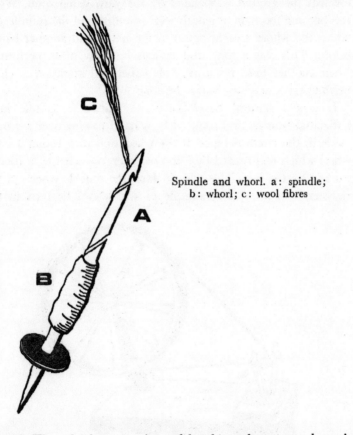

Spindle and whorl. a: spindle;
b: whorl; c: wool fibres

thread. The whorl was a piece of hard wood, stone or bone in annular form through which the spindle was thrust, fitting it near the lower end, to help it to spin. The spindle was from 8-10 in long and had a notch on the end opposite to that on which the whorl was fitted. A large bundle of wool was caught on a stick some 3-4 ft long and held under the arm. Wool fibres

41

were drawn out from this bundle and twisted with the fingers to form a loose thread which was caught under the notch on the spindle. The spindle was then twirled in the fingers, or between the right thigh and the palm of the hand, and allowed to fall towards the ground, suspended by the yarn being spun. When this became too long, a length was wound round the spindle just above the whorl, caught again in the notch and another length begun. This was a long and tedious business, often performed when another task, requiring only superficial attention, such as herding cattle or sheep, had to be done.

It was a natural development to place the spindle in a horizontal bearing and rotate it by a band passing over a groove made in the circumference of the whorl and then round a large wheel which was turned by hand or, later, operated by a treadle worked by the feet. This was, in fact, the muckle wheel, of the eighteenth century, an example of which can be seen in the

The 'muckle wheel'

Museum of Antiquities in Edinburgh. It was also known as the one-thread wheel. As the wheel revolved, the spinner went backwards to supply the wool fibres from a bundle of wool held in the hand, and when a sufficient line of thread was formed, it was wound up on the rotating spindle. This latter process was carried out with difficulty until, c 1800, a flyer was added to the spindle which rotated on it and was driven by a second band

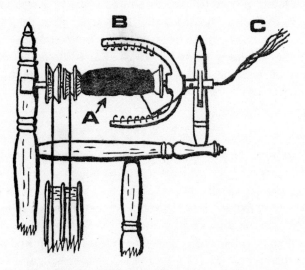

Spindle and flyer on spinning wheel. a: spun yarn on the bobbin; b: flyer, which winds yarn on to the bobbin; c: wool fibres

from the same large main wheel. The flyer had a whorl of different size to that on the spindle, causing it to rotate at a slightly different speed. The difference in speed of rotation, or the amount by which one overtook the other, wound the yarn on the spindle, and thus turned the spinning into a continuous process.

This more complicated arrangement is shown in the above illustration. The yarn was spun on its bobbin rotated by the right-hand pulley; the flyer wound the yarn onto the bobbin; the series of little guide hooks enabled the winding to be

43

controlled by hooking the yarn successively into one after the other and so spreading it along the bobbin. The fibres were oiled to ease the spinning process and to prevent damage to them and they passed through the hollow spindle by which means the twist was controlled; the thickness of the yarn was controlled by the spinner. A modern spinning mule is an adaptation of the simple spindle; a spinning frame is an adaptation of the spindle and flyer. Of the two kinds of yarn needed to make a web of cloth, namely, the warp and the weft, the warp, which runs the full length of the web, must be spun much more strongly to withstand the increased strain to which it is subjected during the process of weaving and also to give greater strength to the resultant cloth.

WARPING

Warping is the process of arranging the warp yarns or threads in the correct order and arrangement to produce the desired colours and pattern in the web. This was a hand process known as stake warping, the stakes being a wooden framework to which were attached numerous pegs round which the yarn was wound with different colours so arranged as to form the required pattern. It was then removed in the form of a running chain and attached to the warp beam, which was turned round and round until all the warp was rolled on to it, to its full length. In the days when Harris Tweed was in its infancy and was little more than a cottage industry producing for home consumption only, the warping was done with only two threads, so that it took almost two days to warp a length of tweed. The warping was originally done by women.

WEAVING

When the warping process was finished, the warped yarn was on the warp beam, that part of the loom which acted as the feed roller. The warp beam was placed in the loom and the ends of the yarn passed through the eyes of the heddles in a manner appropriate to the style of weaving required. The weft having been wound onto small pirns ready for the shuttle, the operator began to weave by manipulating the shuttle from side to side with his right hand, while his left swung the lay backwards and forwards to press the yarn tightly in its place. Both feet were used at the same time on the treadles, raising the heddles in turn to

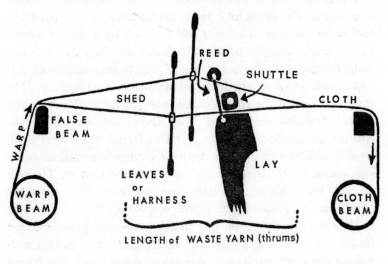

Main weaving parts of loom

form the weave. It took a weaver of good experience upwards of a week, working continuously, to complete a web of tweed. The time taken was of course a function of the amount of yarn provided, the efficiency of the operator, and the complexity of the pattern of the cloth.

The most primitive form of loom was formed by two uprights of wood, a cross beam and a roller at the bottom, on which the cloth was rolled as it was woven, the warp hanging down from the cross-beam. Tension was provided by means of loom-weights of stone or metal. The weft was passed from side to side with a long rod or shuttle and was then driven downwards with a large wooden sword-like stick. In the Western Isles, cloth was woven on the hand loom called the *beairt bheag* (small loom); the shuttle, which was a sheep's shin bone, was thrown by hand.

WAULKING

When the finished web of cloth was removed from the loom, it was generally tough and had a hard feel to it. This harshness had to be changed to softness and closeness by a process known as waulking, fulling or felting. The frame on which the cloth was waulked consisted of a board some 12-20 ft long and about 2 ft wide, with grooves lengthwise along its working surface. The frame was called the *cleith* (wattle) and *cleith-luaidh* (waulking-wattle), probably on account of its having been originally constructed of wattle-work. The waulking-frame was raised upon trestles, while the waulking women were ranged on seats on either side, about 2 ft of space being allowed for each woman. The web of cloth was unrolled and laid along the board, then saturated with ammonia, warm water and soap-suds; then the women worked it vigorously from side to side across the grooves of the frame, slowly moving it lengthwise at the same time, so that each part of the cloth received its due share of attention. The lateral movement of the cloth was sunwise. Occasionally, the waulking-frame was laid on the ground instead of on trestles, the women working the cloth with their feet instead of their hands.

Five major processes were recognised in waulking : the thickening of the cloth; the cleansing; the folding; the process of giving tension to the cloth, and the rite of consecration of the cloth. The waulking was done to the accompaniment of singing. The *bean-luathaidh* (waulking-woman) led the actual work process. The *bean-dhuan* (woman of songs or lilts) led the singing, and the *bean-dhlighe* (woman of ceremony) led the processes in their correct order.

When the thickening of the cloth was completed, the web

was cleaned and washed with plenty of soap in a nearby stream or burn, being carried to and from the water on a hand barrow. After it was washed, it was placed in folds, forming about a square of the cloth, and piled over one another. From these folds the cloth was then rolled slowly and carefully on to a piece of wood, either round or flat; the roll was as hard and as firm as the women could make it, so that the tension of the cloth was evenly distributed. When this process was completed and the end of the web was secured, the whole web was laid across the waulking-frame and the ceremony of consecration began. The first part was solemn in nature; the second was jubilant. Three celebrants took part, the oldest leading and the other two following according to their ages. The first seized the cloth and moved round the frame a half turn. Freeing her hands, she would then seize the web to bring it round one full turn. With the completion of the first move she would say, 'I give a sunwise turn'; with the second turn, to complete the movement, she would add, '. . . dependent on the Father'. The other two women would then give the web one turn each, in the names of the Son and of the Spirit.

Many visitors to the Highlands and Islands have placed on record their observations on the waulking scene. In 1773, during his tour of the Hebrides, Dr Samuel Johnson witnessed a waulking in Skye. His biographer, James Boswell, writes:

Last night Lady Rasey shewed him the operation of wawking cloth, that is thickening it in the same manner as is done by a mill. Here it is performed by women, who kneel upon the ground, and rub it with both their hands, singing an Erse song (a song in Gaelic) all the time. He was asking questions while they were performing this operation, and amidst their loud wild howl, his voice was heard in the room above.

Boswell's description is supplemented by a note in Lockhart's biography (1837) of Sir Walter Scott:

We heard the women singing as they waulked the cloth by rubbing it with their hands and feet, and screaming all the while in a sort of chorus. At a distance the sound was wild and sweet enough, but rather discordant when you approached too near the performers.

Thomas Pennant, during his tour of Scotland and the Hebrides (1772), also mentions the waulking process, this time as it was done by the feet of the waulking women:

Twelve or fourteen women divided into two equal numbers, sit down on each side of a board ribbed lengthways, placing the cloth on it: first they begin to work it backwards and forwards with their hands, singing at the same time, as at the quern: when they have tired their hands, every female uses her feet for the same purpose, and six or seven pairs of naked feet are in the most violent agitation, working one against the other: as by this time they grow very earnest in their labours, the fury of the song rises; at length it arrives to such a pitch, that without breach of charity you would imagine a troop of female daemoniacs to have been assembled.

A most detailed description of waulking occurs in Frances Tolmie's collection of Gaelic songs from the Western Islands. In her notes to the collection, under the heading of 'A Singer's memories of life in Skye', she refers to a certain Mary Ross, born in 1848:

Mary remembers the first time she assisted at a waulking, when another girl and she were placed beside a remarkable old woman, who was to take the leading part in the singing, but was not expected to touch the cloth. They sat one on each side to support her, at about the middle of the board, while she poured forth one song after another; occasionally, according to the custom, adding witty or satirical or amusing lines applicable to members of the audience. Young men were there, as usual, and even grave elderly men did not think it beneath their dignity to be present when this woman, possessed of a wonderful memory and knowledge of fine passages of ancient poetry, was to sing. It was believed that her mother, a native of Lewis, and full of lore, had imparted it all to her, together with her skill in certain magical practices for which the people of Lewis were renowned. A waulking, while a useful and necessary domestic function, was also regarded as a pleasant form of entertainment. Invitations were issued, and the obliging guests came dressed neatly and specially for the occasion, with bare arms and stout aprons. They took their places—six to ten persons on each side, leaving elbow-room—at the waulking table. This was a long board about three feet in width, grooved lengthways, and resting on trestles. The cloth to be fulled or thickened was slowly dealt out from a vat at one end of the board. This vat, which contained a special liquid, was presided over by the good-wife of the house or some other persons of experience.

The mass of cloth was firmly grasped by one of the waulkers and pushed towards the person opposite, who with a similar gesture returned it to be sent on to the next opposing pair. This process continued until the cloth had gone the round of the board three or four times. When the moisture in it had been duly absorbed, the cloth was plunged again into the vat to get a drink and go the round of the board again until pronounced thick enough, singing accompanied the process throughout, songs of slow and solemn character coming first, followed by those in quicker time and merrier. Towards the close a slow measure was again used. The new web received its final treatment to the accompaniment of a solemn strain of song. During the singing of it the cloth was slowly and carefully wound round a board used to press it and give it a finish.

49

In another description by Marjory Kennedy Fraser, we learn something of the songs and the stimulating influence of the singing on the waulking process :

> As this process of fulling the cloth was long and heavy, the songs used for it were correspondingly stimulating. And many ancient airs are still preserved in Benbecula just because the work of weaving still goes busily forward there. A much larger crofter community than that of Eriskay— there were some 1000 folk in the Isle of Benbecula—hardly a day passes that is not marked by a waulking. And where there are many waulkings there will survive the greater number of varied and complex labour song refrains. For at these gatherings the singing is the attraction, and the tedious work of tossing, dumping and circulating the moisture-laden cloth is completely forgotten in the intoxicating swing of the body to the rhythmic refrain. The refrains are sung by the whole company, but there is interest also in the verse lines, which are given by the leader only.

The St Kildans were reported (in 1727) to 'thicken their cloth upon stakes or rods or mats of hay twisted or woven together in small ropes; they worked hard at this employment, first making use of their hands and at last of their feet; and when they are at work they commonly sing all the time, one of their number acting the part of a prime chantress, whom all the rest follow and obey'.

A description of more recent date (c 1910) is that of Miss Annie Johnston of Barra, who had a great store of the Gaelic tradition passed on to her by her mother :

> When the web of cloth came home from the loom, they used to decide which night they would have for the waulking. There was the food to be prepared, fresh butter, oatcakes and barley cakes to be made, whisky to be brought

home, crowdy and *gruthim* to be made, a hen or two to be killed and prepared, and then a word to be sent to the waulking women. There would be a host, and the waulking-board was in his care. This was usually made of wooden planks put together, or else, if they had none, a door would do. The number of waulking women was according to the size of the cloth, and if it was blue cloth there had to be two teams, working in turn, to make it really tight. Usually five or six was the number that could sit on each side of the waulking-board. The women used to come, with calico petticoats, drugget coats and tibbet aprons. Then the hostess used to baptize the cloth, that is, she shook Holy Water on it in the name of the Trinity, and put it in a tub of urine. They used to say nothing was so good for taking out the oil as urine. They used to take it out of the tub and put it on the board, and doubled it on the board. Then the woman who was best at singing began with a slow song, and then a warming-up song, and after that a short light song to encourage them because they were getting tired.

After this, the hostess would measure the cloth with her middle finger, and usually there was not much shrinking in it at the first three songs. Then another one would begin; she would sing three songs too, and as the cloth had been warmed up by the first three songs, it would shrink more at the second attempt, and at the third attempt it ought to be ready, if it were a blanket or white cloth. At first it was eight finger-lengths (ells) broad. When the cloth was ready it would be three inches narrower in breadth anyway. If it were blue cloth, that is, the cloth the men wore on board the boats, it would be much thicker, and another band of waulkers would need to go to the board when the first band was tired. When the cloth was as thick as desired, the women then used to put it on the *coinneal*, ie, roll it up in a roll, and sing an *oran basaidh* (clapping song). Clapping songs were usually light and funny such as :

51

'Who will I take with me on the Irish ship?
Ho my sweetheart, he my sweetheart,'

and so on.

I never heard them have a blessing in Barra, though I asked many people about it, but one of the waulking women would say to the host, if the cloth were for him : 'Enjoy and use it, pay the dance, and throw across the next cloth'. If it were for a young man : 'Enjoy and use it, tear and rend it, and marry before it wears out'. Then the waulking women used to wash themselves, and come in for food and a dram, and the young men used to put the waulking-board out into the barn, and the young folk would collect for a dance.

Interesting comparisons can be made between the process of waulking as it was performed in the Western Isles and elsewhere in Europe. An Orkney waulking ceremony is described by John Firth (1922) :

This was a part of the business that the whole family shared in simultaneously. A door was placed on a small dining table for eight persons to sit around. The *claith*, wrung by hand out of the same evil-smelling liquid as the dyes were dissolved in, was laid, steaming hot, on the improvised table; and the people seated around pulled, rubbed and twisted the web round and around, always taking care that the circular motion was in accordance with the path of the sun. After an hour of this work, the web was measured with an ellwand, and if not found to be sufficiently shrunk the operation was renewed. A good deal of boisterous but good-humoured mirth and sport was indulged in during this waulking o' the web.

Firth does not say that songs were sung, but it may be assumed that singing went along with at least some part of the process; rhythm nearly always engenders song.

Page 53: (above) Beaming a tweed, a mill process; (below) weaver tying-in a tweed.

Page 54: (above) Weaver setting up a tweed; (below) hand-loom weaver on a Hattersley loom.

The waulking or fulling of cloth by stamping or other violent action is an ancient craft. It is mentioned by Seneca as *'saltus Salaris aut fullonius'*, thus comparing the waulker's stamping to the weapon dance of the Salients, a Roman clerical corporation. Waulking was usually done with the cloth immersed in a vat filled with a hot solution, the waulker using his feet to stamp the material. This method was used in places as far apart as Italy and Sweden. At the felting of woollen socks, the Faroese women used to stand and stamp in a tub filled with urine.

In Sweden another method was used, known as lying waulking. In the parish of Föra in Öland (an island in the Baltic) the method is described: 'The suits of the men had a short jacket of home-waulked frieze-cloth, which was waulked in boiling hot water and placed into the bottomless barrel, which was placed on top of one of the long benches. Then a farmhand and a servant girl lay down on opposite sides of the bench, put their feet into the barrel and started kicking the cloth'. Lying waulking was also practised in Norway and Iceland where a bottomless barrel was also used.

Finland also had the tub-stamping method of waulking the cloth which was placed in a long trough filled with hot soapy water. The trough's ends were formed as seats with sloping backs for the waulkers. Boards on the sides prevented the cloth falling down to the floor. The two waulkers, either men or women, sat opposite each other with bare feet, and stamped the cloth which was soaked with hot soapy water at intervals. The waulking took a long time, sometimes several days, after which the cloth was stretched out to dry.

Though the waulking was a time for story-telling and singing, there does not seem to have been a tradition of waulking songs to match the Hebridean genre. Among the original Swedish rural population of Finland, waulking seems to have taken place to the accompaniment of singing. A song recorded in 1900 was collected during a waulking, though it could have been for cloth, wool, or socks. Called *Valkan vison* (waulking song), it ran:

The Old Ways

Roll of cloth, roll of cloth.
Bundle of wool, bundle of wool,
tight as the wall,
smooth as the egg,
thick as the bum of the
pastor's wife.

3 The Beginnings of Expansion

A GROWING MARKET

WHEN Martin Martin visited the Hebrides and printed an account of his observations about 1595, Hebridean exports included cattle, hides, wool, and some plaiding; these were destined for mainland markets. The islands were able to support a population of some 40,000 in reasonable comfort. Though the diet of the Islanders may not have been very varied, the Hebrideans were, if Martin is reliable, fairly well clothed. Cloth-making was a general skill, performed almost exclusively by women, with no individual district reaching such perfection as to merit special outside attention.

With the advent of the nineteenth century, however, there were signs that the women of Harris were beginning to pull ahead in the production of cloth goods of outstanding quality. These goods were, however, mainly for domestic consumption, or else made for those within the community, who paid in services or kind of a different nature. The material would then be made into suits and garments by the community's tailors. It has been suggested that though the cloth was of uneven quality, it was accepted because there was at that time (c 1825) no direct competition from machine-made goods brought across from the Scottish mainland. There was, however, a subtle form of competition. Travellers to and from the mainland sported clothing which

57

was bound to be compared with the local-made stuff, exciting a desire for better material. Perhaps this was the stimulus which resulted in the women of Harris becoming known for their skill in cloth-making. As yet the cloth was called *clo mor*; Tweed had still to come. With the production of a better quality cloth, a small home market was probably created, and this would have been encouraged by the fact that the folk tended to specialise in their trades and so became dependent on others for what they might once have produced for themselves. Such trades were boat-building, fishing, tailoring, shoemaking, sail and net making, weaving, and the like.

By the end of the 1840s, Harris had become well known for the excellence of its weaving. The first piece of tweed recognised as such is said to have been sold by two sisters, Marion and Christina MacLeod, born on the island of Pabbay, in the Sound of Harris, about 1810 to 1815. About 1845 they went to Strond, in south Harris. The family was exceptional in possessing two looms, and their substantial production of cloth earned them the nickname of the 'Paisley Sisters', a reference to the Paisley shawl industry which was beginning to expand at that time; they had also received training in weaving at Paisley.

In 1835, the Harris estate, held for centuries by its traditional clan owners, the MacLeods of Harris, who had their seat at Dunvegan in Skye, passed into the hands of the Earl of Dunmore for £60,000. The Earl held the estate for a few short years but died in 1843, leaving a widow and an infant son. His widow, the Dowager Catherine Herbert, a daughter of the Earl of Leicester, took a keen interest in her Harris estate. In particular, she was quick to notice the quality of tweeds made by the Harris crofters' wives, and which showed great scope for improvement. Directions were given to some weavers to copy the Murray tartan in tweed, and in 1846, so tradition has it, she bought the first full length of tweed. The cloth was made up into suiting for keepers and gillies, the Dowager was delighted with it, and furthermore she realised that the material had sales potential.

There were many initial difficulties to be overcome before an external market could be won, for comparison with machine-made cloths was still to the detriment of the home-made product. The first tweeds of the Harris type seem to have been rather pronounced checks, rough in texture, and uneven in quality. Dyeing, spinning and weaving, all performed as manual processes, produced only too often irregularities in the cloth. As a start, the Dowager arranged for a number of Harris girls to leave their native village of Strond to go to Alloa, to learn there the weaving of more intricate patterns. She paid their expenses during their training period, thus anticipating today's acknowledgment of the value of the residential training course. That this move was in the right direction was evidenced by the fact that by the late 1840s tweeds were being sent to customers in faraway London. These customers were, at first, aristocratic; they were quick to see the advantages of the cloth for outdoor wear, particularly in sporting pursuits: it was warm, reasonably light, and 'turned' light rain. Without doubt, the increasing use of Highland estates for sporting activities helped to increase the demand for tweed, or Harris Tweed, as it came to be known.

The obvious success of the Harris Tweeds was noted in other parts of the Highlands. One reason for this was the sufferings of the Highland population from 1836 to about 1848, the result of crop failures and the evictions from good land to poor land hardly able to yield sufficient food for a family. Naturally thoughts turned to other measures of support, and enterprising, philanthropic persons, such as Harriet, Duchess of Sutherland, organised home industries, of which cloth-making was one.

Meanwhile, in Harris, the success in sales of Harris Tweed brought further developments. In 1857, Lady Dunmore began a stocking and embroidery industry, for which an instructress was brought to the island and a workroom built. This development was helped by another enterprising woman who came on the Hebridean scene, a Mrs Thomas, wife of Captain Thomas, RN, who was with the Ordnance Survey Department and engaged on surveying work in the islands at the time. Mrs Thomas' interest began when she had a pair of stockings presented to her by a Harris woman. Realising that most of the sales efforts were on the side of tweed, she thought to procure orders for the knitted goods. In 1859, or perhaps a little later, she opened an agency at her home in Edinburgh for the sale of both tweeds and knitted goods and, by her efforts, a sizeable market was created in that city.

The tweed and knitting industry expanded. At one time, there were some 400 people engaged in knitting in Harris alone. The crofters in the southern isles also began to take an active part in tweed-making and knitting; about 1877, South Uist tweeds found their way to the London market. And across the Minch the crofters in Skye were also participants in the growing activity, the industry there being helped along by the interest of MacLeod of MacLeod, the proprietor. In South Uist, Lady Gordon Cathcart, who owned the island together with Benbecula and Barra, acted as agent for tweeds produced by her tenants and sent by her to Messrs Parfitt of Jermyn Street, London. This firm, sensing the pulse of the market, sent patterns up to Uist to be both copied and improved; records indicate that they were well pleased with the Uisteachs' ability to satisfy the market demand. There were, however, occasional pieces of tweed which had serious defects, often as a result of accident, and the fact that webs of cloth were not made to a multiple of suit- or coat-lengths caused considerable wastage.

In all this development of the tweed-making industry, Lewis was conspicuous by its absence. There were reasons for this. In 1844 Sir James Matheson had purchased Lewis from the Sea-forth family and soon after found that his tenants were in sore need of his bottomless pocket. Destitution was rife among the Lewis folk and, rather than give mere handouts, he organised activities for the men which would improve the Lewis estate. He advanced some £33,000 for meal and seed potatoes, and, in addition, large sums were laid out to provide direct employment on roads, bridges, shooting lodges and industrial buildings, including a brickworks and a chemical works for the extraction of paraffin from peat. Much of this work was unskilled and well fitted to the untrained Lewismen who made up Matheson's labour pools. The work, however, was not of a permanently productive nature, though it did increase the island's facilities—people could now travel dry-shod on roads and over rivers, instead of having to make more hazardous journeys across the moors. When Sir James died in 1878, all his improvements came to a standstill, and soon after the extent to which the Lewis crofters had depended on his works became apparent. In addition, about the time of Matheson's death, the Lewis fishing industry, which had developed into a healthy state, was upset by the introduction of fish sales by auction instead of by private contract between fishermen and curers. Altogether, the Lewis crofters found themselves in an unfavourable position and looked around for some outlet into which they could direct their energies to create at least a semblance of economic stability for themselves. They looked to the south, to Harris, and saw the state of the flourishing tweed industry there. It is stated that the first web of tweed made in Lewis for sale outside the island appeared in 1881. The parish of Lochs, being geographically nearer to Harris, was the first district to take up the making of tweed; again some impetus was given by the interest shown by a local lady.

THE HOME INDUSTRIES MOVEMENT

The product from Lewis was, like its Harris counterpart, wholly hand-made, and the Lewis cloth appeared on the market, not unnaturally, as Harris Tweed. In due course, the other parishes in Lewis took up the production of cloth for external, commercial consumption, though the progress was slow, mainly because Lewismen had found another competitive outlet for their energies in the herring fishing, which was just coming into its heyday. During these formative years a two-headed pattern for sales was emerging. First there were the small merchants on the islands who either bought webs of cloth for sale on the mainland, or who exchanged goods for the cloth instead of cash. Local merchants often encourage production by buying wool and yarn, and supplying these to crofters who wove cloth in return for cash, though mainly for credit and kind.

Secondly, there were the outlets provided by non-profit-making groups such as the Scottish Home Industries Association. Another much smaller market for tweeds was open to any producer who could establish a sales contact, mostly through a tourist or visitor connection, not only in London but in other parts of the British Isles. A typical merchant who created his own sales outlets was Norman MacLeod of Tarbert in Harris, who had contacts with various wholesale houses in 1879. The price he obtained for the tweed was from 4s to 6s per yard, for cloth which was made from hand-carded wool, hand-spun yarn and hand-woven. However the main credit for sowing the early seeds of industrial organisation must go to the philanthropic bodies which pro-liferated throughout the Highlands and Islands towards the latter decades of the nineteenth century.

In April 1849, Harriet, Duchess of Sutherland established an Industrial Society, with headquarters at Golspie. In the following year an exhibition of home crafts was held at which sufficient profit was made from the sale of the exhibits to show that the continuation of the society would be of benefit to the country folk. In time Sutherland Home Industries was founded.

In 1889 the Scottish Home Industries Association was estab-lished, under the patronage of Princess Louise; the president was the Countess of Roseberry. The objects of the association were to find a market for the products of home industries; to improve the quality of the goods by providing instruction and circulating information; and to pay the workers a fair price for their labour. It was also recognised that 'it was only as a self-supporting business that the success, or even the permanent existence, of the Associa-tion could be permanently secured'. A depot was established in

London, and four branches were created, one of which, the Northern Counties Branch, covered the home-industry activities in the Hebrides.

In the same year, 1889, another body, The Highland Home Industries & Arts Association was established, embracing the counties of Inverness, Ross, Cromarty, Sutherland, Caithness, Elgin and Banff. The association had the following to offer as its *raison d'être*:

> It may be that the hand cannot compete with the machine when rapidity of production and immediate profit are aimed at; but there is undoubtedly a growing appreciation of home-made fabrics; and, in some districts of the Highlands, the manufacture of tweeds and the knitting of stockings are even now engaged in profitably, and a market for the products is found through ordinary commercial channels. It cannot be doubted, however, than many industries, which within quite recent times were practised in every cottage, are fast falling into disuse, and that the time which used to be devoted to them is lost or wasted. It is equally beyond doubt that the revival of such industries would greatly promote thrift and add to the comfort and to the self-respect of the poorer classes of people engaged in agricultural and pastoral occupations. By the working up of the wool in the home, time now lost would be filled by healthy and interesting occupations, the artistic faculty of the race would be revived and stimulated, the money now spent in getting these materials worked up elsewhere, or in the purchase of inferior articles, would be saved, and better fabrics for dress and other home uses, better domestic utensils, and more comfortable homes would result.

This body differed from the Scottish Home Industries Association in that it did not propose to establish any shop or commercial organisation, but to effect its purpose by obtaining sales at exhibitions. Other small societies with similar aims and objects were established. In time, however, the philanthropic bodies found that though they were fairly successful in the creation of markets, the difficulty of financing the workers remained.

Two conflicting points of view were discussed at the close of the nineteenth century. First, events had shown the need for a commercial organisation and considerable working capital. The people who made the tweed had neither, and if they were left wholly in the hands of the merchants they were at a disadvantage, partly in being unable to hold out for a good price and partly by their involvement in the truck system, whereby woven cloth was exchanged for goods or credit and no cash transaction took place. The second viewpoint held that, at the usual price for tweed, the workers received little enough for their labours and that any large organisation brought into existence would require part of the retail price for the cloth to subsidise itself. The upshot was that the Scottish Home Industries Association became a limited company, registered in 1896 with a nominal capital of £10,000 on which dividends were limited to 3 per cent, and a new selling agency, named The Crofters' Agency, was started by Mrs Stewart MacKenzie of Seaforth and given a depot in London. Mrs Stewart MacKenzie was later to become Lady Seaforth, a name which had once been important in Lewis (it was from the Seaforth family that Sir James Matheson had bought Lewis in 1844). At the same time, the Scottish Home Industries Association established a depot in London, with others in Tarbert in Harris, and Stornoway in Lewis. The association also appointed a travelling inspector with a view to improving the quality of the tweeds.

Both the Scottish Home Industries Association and the Crofters' Agency found some problems, stemming largely from the truck system, in the working of their island depots. Depot managers were instructed 'to pay for all purchases of tweed in cash, leaving it entirely to the option of the crofters whether they will or not make purchases of groceries, wool, or other commodities which the stores offer for sale'. It was found that some of the people who dealt with the Tarbert depot were so poor that they were often in want of wool or necessities between the time they began to make a web of cloth and the finishing of it and thus it was often judged necessary to advance such commodities as wool, dyes, meal and sugar. The Crofters' Agency advanced wool only and it bought cloth for cash.

By the time the nineteenth century closed, Harris Tweed had made a name for itself. Half a century of external sales had put the cloth on the map in a market built up by the endeavours of both individuals and organisations. Paradoxically, while the attraction of selling a wholly hand-made product had been maintained and strengthened in Harris and Lewis it had dwindled on the Highland mainland because of the stiff competition from small local mills.

Another factor which helped to fix the public eye on Harris Tweed was the idea that the hand-made product was better than its machine-made equivalent. Since 1862, John Ruskin had been preaching the educational, social and artistic advantages of handwork. To this movement William Morris, with his definite ideas about the industrialisation of society, contributed some practical, though perhaps not commercially-viable examples. The principle was one which excited sympathy and tended to lend an extra dimension to Harris Tweed. It already had a glamour about it. Towards the end of the nineteenth century an interest was being taken in folklore and folksongs; in the British Isles, in Europe and in America, collectors were at work. The Hebrides became a happy hunting ground for such collectors, among whom Marjorie Kennedy Fraser was perhaps the best known. Her *Songs of the Hebrides* swept across the world and contributed to a desire for things of the past which became almost a 'rage'. In Ireland too, at the turn of the century, writers like Yeats and Lady Gregory were paying homage to their Celtic background. Books appeared, at popular prices, describing the people of the Western Isles as living anachronisms existing in primitive conditions with a culture and language of their own. All in all, by a

65

happy coincidence, Harris Tweed was a child of its time and benefited thereby. The 'Celtic twilight' era had begun and ushered in the 'we in dreams behold the Hebrides' phase. This, coupled with the cloth being made in thatched 'black houses', thick with the reek of a peat fire, and use of natural vegetable dyes picked from moor and shore, made a product which was almost a status symbol to buy. Nor was this all. Tweeds being produced by hand from wool to web tended to vary one from the other, and a pattern could never be matched exactly, particularly in its colouring; so the cloth had all the appeal of exclusiveness. In sum, by its own particular characteristics, Harris Tweed at once created its market and its problems. As the demand for the cloth increased, so did the supply fail to meet it. Two questions arose : must the cloth remain available only to those who could afford it, or could something be done to increase production while still retaining the basic characteristics of Harris Tweed?

Two opposing opinions were voiced. One said that Harris Tweed must remain for all time a cloth produced wholly by hand, more or less custom-built, even though this might eventually price it outside a large market. The other opinion was based on a more rational approach to the problem of meeting demand, namely that a certain amount of speed-up in cloth production was required and that this did not necessarily mean that the methods used to increase production would result in a cloth in any way inferior to the wholly hand-made cloth. In time, what took place was the elimination of two bottlenecks and the introduction of processes to remove some of the drudgery associated with the early stages in the manufacture of the cloth : carding and spinning mills were established.

THE CONGESTED DISTRICTS BOARD

In 1897 the Congested Districts (Scotland) Act was passed and fathered the Congested Districts Board, which came into close contact with the bodies responsible for home-industry activities

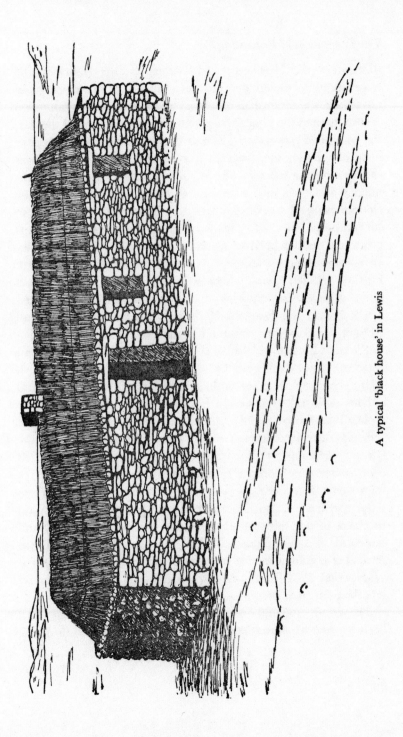

A typical 'black house' in Lewis

throughout the Highlands and Islands. In the Hebrides, the tweed industry, though operated on a fairly widespread scale, had no semblance of formal industrial or commercial organisation and so merited the board's attention. Under Section 4 of the Act, the board had powers, *inter alia*, to expend money in the development of spinning and weaving in congested districts. A sum was earmarked for a scheme of practical instruction to improve cloth-making in Lewis and a committee of local persons under the chairmanship of Sheriff Campbell in Stornoway was set up to supervise this work. After exploratory investigations a report was produced on the basis of which an instructor, Mr Alexander Lamont, was appointed with a salary provided by the board. Further detailed investigations were carried out and two main points emerged as requiring urgent attention. First, the tweed workers were handicapped by being able to make only small webs of tweed. Secondly, there was the risk of irregular colouring in the cloth because only small pots were available for dyeing, and these could not dye in one batch sufficient wool for a full-length web. To meet this latter problem two large boilers, each of 30 gallons capacity, were sent to Uig on the west coast of Lewis.

The board encouraged improvements to the looms already in use, with the introduction of the flying shuttle instead of the hand-thrown one. This improved loom was the foot-operated *beairt-mhor* (big loom). Interest-free loans were offered for improvement and for the purchase of improved looms. These latter cost from £6 to £8 each and payments were arranged on the basis of one-third in advance, one-third in six months, and one-third in twelve months. That the weaving of tweed was profitable is shown by the repayment figures. During the seven-year period 1902-9 only £1 for a loom, and 8s for a spinning wheel remained outstanding.

The embryonic industry in general now felt the stage had been reached when mechanisation had to be seriously considered.

THE INTRODUCTION OF MILL PROCESSES

The first process to receive attention from the production aspect was that of carding. Until about the mid-1890s, carding had been almost entirely done by hand. It was not only a slow task, but an extremely tiring one and, when the work of the croft had to be kept going at the same time, the output of hand-carded wool was not particularly high, at least not high enough to meet the grow-

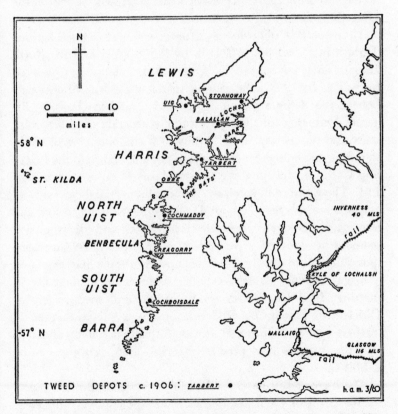

Location diagram, showing also the tweed depots of the non-profitmaking agencies, c 1906—ie at the end of the first phase of the industry's development

69

ing demand for wool ready for spinning. Some crofters had, in fact, been sending wool to the mainland to have it carded at mills there, and some spinning was also done on the mainland, with the result that in some tweeds marketed as Harris Tweed the only hand-process was the weaving. But while it was beginning to be accepted that the carding stage at any rate could be speeded up by a mill, it was obvious that any work done on the mainland would debase the unwritten specification which Harris Tweed had established for itself over some fifty years, namely, that it was a cloth produced, in all its stages, if not in Harris, at least in the Outer Hebrides.

To meet this difficulty a carding mill was erected outside Tarbert in Harris in 1900, built by the proprietor of the North Harris estate, Sir Samuel E. Scott; the machinery was powered by water. In 1903 a Stornoway merchant, Aneas MacKenzie, bought the defunct Patent Slip, which had been built by Sir James Matheson for the repair and construction of sailing ships when Stornoway was in its heyday as a shipping port of world significance, and there erected a carding mill, known as the Patent Slip Carding Mill (now the site of Messrs S. A. Newall & Sons Ltd). These two mills increased the amount of island-carded wool available to spinners in both Lewis and Harris for conversion into yarn; production of tweed increased and demand was temporarily satisfied. In their turn, however, the increased quantities of the cloth which now appeared on the market caused a bigger demand, which even the spinners found difficulty in meeting. In 1904 another small carding mill was erected, at Diricleit in Harris, by Roderick Smith, a sub-postmaster at Tarbert who dealt in tweeds. It was gradually becoming apparent that the investment of private capital in plant was going to be worthwhile.

The increased demand resulted in the opening of more depots by the Scottish Home Industries Association at Uig in Lewis, Obbe in Harris, Lochboisdale in South Uist, and at Creagorry Pier in Benbecula. It also resulted in Lewis weavers taking the

Page 71: (above) Greasy webs waiting by the roadside for collection by a producer's vehicle; (below) hand-loom weaver at work.

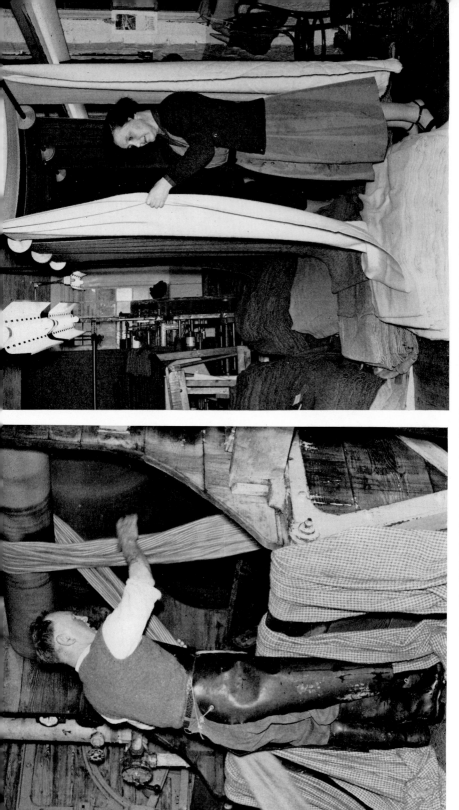

Page 72: (left) Washing greasy webs; (right) examination of finished tweed for flaws.

initiative in stepping-up production to satisfy the demand for Harris Tweed. In 1899 there had been about 55 looms in Lewis and 200 in Harris. In 1906 there were 161 looms in Lewis; in 1911 there were 300. This involved an interesting social development in that although, in Harris, women remained largely responsible for the output of cloth, in Lewis male weavers became predominant largely because of the wider introduction there of the flying-shuttle which required greater strength and stamina. According to estimates made at the time, production of cloth in 1903 was valued at £8,000, in 1904 at £15,000; in 1905 at £20,460. The average wholesale price was 2s 8d per yard; the retail price varied from 4s 6d to 7s 6d, depending on the type of tweed.

By 1903 it was reported that the weavers were unable to supply the whole of the demand for tweed. But other reports were of over-production. The unexpected rise in the output of the cloth from Lewis caused much concern, since it was obvious that to attain such unprecedented output, some mill-spun yarn had to be used. There was growing resentment at the provision of mill-carding and mill-spinning facilities (spinning had been added to the Patent Slip Mill at Stornoway), but it was argued with some justification that at least these processes were done on the island and satisfied the definition of island-made.

In 1902 Lewis was visited by royalty. King Edward VII and Queen Alexandra landed at Stornoway and with commendable initiative and with more than an eye to good publicity, some tweed was presented to them. The gift was accepted and, unlike many gifts made to royalty, was put to good use as suitings. Whether the cloth in question was Harris Tweed or what was then being called 'Lewis Tweed' is not certain. Probably, considering the status of the recipients, it was a wholly hand-made product. This royal patronage boosted the Lewis product and when the King died in 1910, the weavers of Balallan in Lewis sent a letter of condolence to King George V, expressing gratitude for the interest which his father had taken in the cloth by visiting

E

an exhibition put on in London by the Scottish Home Industries Association and buying a few suit lengths at a time when tweed was temporarily out of favour.

The interest in Harris Tweed was not of course confined to royalty. In 1906 a Henry Lyons of London was convicted of a contravention of Section 2 of the Merchandise Marks Act for selling as Harris Tweed a suit made from cloth mill-spun and power-loomed in Huddersfield. The extent of the accused's fraud and effrontery was equalled only by the loudness of his lamentations on being convicted. This prosecution was instituted at the behest of the Scottish Home Industries Association, which had managed to stir the Board of Trade into activity on the industry's behalf. The trial tended to emphasise that Harris Tweed was a cloth made entirely in the Hebrides and turned the thoughts of those directly connected with the growing industry towards taking suitable steps to unite to protect it.

FIRST STEPS TO UNITY

These steps were not going to be easy however, for there were on the market a number of cloths classed as Harris Tweed. Harris was the main producer of the wholly hand-made article; Lewis, on the other hand, was responsible for a mill-carded, mill-spun, but hand-woven cloth. By 1907 the Lewis weavers relied so much on mill-spun yarn that the amount of hand-spun tweed did not justify the expenses of the Scottish Home Industries Association depots in Lewis, so these were gradually closed. On the other hand, the Crofters' Agency kept open its Balallan, Lewis depot. Sharp practices continued. Some crofters collaborated so that guarantees were issued stating that the cloth produced was hand-spun, hand-woven, and sometimes even hand-carded as well, and these guarantees were attached to mill-spun webs of cloth called Stornoway Tweed which was of inferior quality and which damaged the genuine article. With mill-spun yarn available, an increasing number of merchants were buying up yarn, warping it and putting it out for weaving and hand finishing on a commission basis; the yarn and the resulting cloth remained the property of the merchants, who eventually became known as the Lewis producers, and who sometimes used mill-spun warp and hand-spun weft, and sometimes no hand-spun wool at all. This mill-spun cloth enabled the Lewis production completely to outstrip the Harris output in the decade up to 1910.

In 1911 it was calculated that the cost of production of a tweed, made wholly of machine-spun yarn, but hand-woven and hand-finished was between 1s 9d and 1s 10d per yard, and if passed off as Harris Tweed it made a profit of about 1s per yard, or nearly £3 per web. The profit to the producer of a genuine tweed was very much less, though the cloth sold for 6s to 7s per yard.

In Harris, the temptation to use mill-spun yarn was great and it did appear in tweeds produced for sale or exchange to merchants. The latter, in order to protect themselves against charges of misrepresentation, began to demand a guarantee from the weavers that the tweeds supplied were genuine hand-made articles. A Form of Declaration was drawn up :

I hereby guarantee that the length of tweed as described below is entirely hand-spun, hand-woven, and home-dyed Harris Tweed.

Signature ....

Address ....

Description of Tweed (Colour and Design)

....

No : ....

Despite this filter system, tweeds which did not comply with the declaration still found their way to the market. From 1906 onwards a series of meetings of interested parties took place in Stornoway, Harris and other parts of the Outer Hebrides to consider what steps should be taken to protect the wholly hand-made tweed. The obvious step was to obtain a trade mark, but

75

there were differences of opinion as to what the trade mark should cover.

At this time there were two main agencies in London; the Scottish Home Industries Association, headed by the Duchess of Sutherland, and the Crofters' Agency, represented by Mrs Stewart MacKenzie. In Harris, some producers had formed themselves into the Harris Tweed Association and objected to the Lewis producers using the name Harris Tweed at all, even for the wholly hand-made product. Mrs MacKenzie sympathised with this viewpoint. On the other hand, the Duchess of Sutherland took the broader view that the name Harris Tweed should be applied to the wholly hand-made product, irrespective of whichever part of the Outer Hebrides produced it. This was the view held by those Stornoway merchants, associated with the hand-made article, who had formed themselves into the Lewis Harris Tweed Association. Eventually a conference was held in Inverness on 16 March 1907, attended by the Duchess, the leading Stornoway traders in home-spun tweed, and other individuals. The following resolution was adopted:

> That in view of the desirability of having one trade mark established for the tweed made in the Long Island, or Outer Hebrides, and known as 'Harris Tweed', it is unanimously agreed to unite with the Scottish Home Industries Association in having the proposed trade mark passed by the Board of Trade, and the meeting expresses the hope that Mrs MacKenzie of Seaforth will also join in this matter.

The view expressed in the resolution was eventually accepted by both Mrs MacKenzie on behalf of the Crofters' Agency, and the Harris producers, though not before competing applications for trade marks had been made to the Board of Trade. Mrs MacKenzie had, early in 1907, obtained a registered trade mark for 'Hand Spun Hand Woven Tweeds (in the piece) in Harris and Long Islands (Outer Hebrides) Wool'. This was the Seagull trade mark. Not unnaturally, the Harris producers feared the result of having one trade mark to cover the whole of the Outer Hebrides. They argued that producers in Lewis, and particularly the Lewis spinners, might find an excuse to market the product of mill-spun yarn as Harris Tweed. This fear had been given foundation by the erection by Kenneth MacKenzie in 1906 of the carding and spinning mill in Stornoway, and the extension in 1908 of the Patent Slip Carding Mill to include spinning facilities.

In the end, differences were set aside and two measures were decided upon. The first was the formation of a body of association; the second was the application for a standardisation mark (now called a certification trade mark) for the hand-made article produced in the Outer Hebrides and legitimately described and marketed as Harris Tweed.

The provisions relating to the standardisation trade marks were at that time contained in Section 2 of the Trade Marks Act 1905 as follows:

Where any association or person undertakes the examination of any goods in respect of origin, material, mode of manufacture, quality, accuracy, or other characteristic, and certifies the result of such examination by mark used upon in connexion with such goods, the Board of Trade may, if they shall judge it to be to the public advantage, permit such association or person to register such mark as a trade mark in respect of such goods, whether or not such association or person be a trading association or trader possessed of a goodwill in connexion with such examination and certifying. When so registered such trade mark shall be deemed in all respects to be a registered trade mark, and such association or person to be the proprietor thereof, save that such trade mark shall be transmissible or assignable only by permission of the Board of Trade.

4 Growing Up

PRODUCTION METHODS AND COSTS

AT this point it is useful to review the methods and economics of the production of Harris Tweed in the early formative years of the twentieth century. The wholly hand-made product was still a genuine follow-on from the age-old methods of making the cloth. Little had changed, except perhaps in the matter of synthetic dyes.

In 1856 had come the discovery of the first synthetic dyestuff by Perkin, a young chemist—who was in fact trying to discover a new method of producing quinine. He obtained a black substance which by mistake he boiled in alcohol; to his amazement, the resulting fluid stained everything it touched a bright violet colour. He consulted several dyers, in particular Pullars of Perth, and later began the manufacture of the first aniline dyestuff, 'Perkin's Mauve'. This was followed by other dyes, the most important of which was magenta.

In 1876 Peter Griess discovered the diazo reaction which made possible the manufacture of a large range of colours. Then came the synthesis of alizarine which supplanted the old madder root, hitherto the only source of a really satisfactory red dye. Immediately a large range of colours of superior fastness to natural dyes became available. About 1887, azo dyes, as they were known, were actually produced on the fibre, involving a new principle in dyeing, and changing the dyer into an actual colour-maker. The tendency now was to use these synthetic dyes, which were prepared ready for use and available at the depots of the selling agencies in the islands. This was not altogether regarded as being a debasement of the final product. Harris Tweeds had built up a justifiable reputation for being extremely long-wearing and this introduced a problem in the prevention of colour-fading as the years went by; certain vegetable dyes had proved themselves not to be as light-fast as customers required. Vegetable dyeing was, of course, still practised, but it had to be done with extreme care : in fact only those with the old traditional methods of dyeing at their fingertips were able to produce colour-fast dyes from plants. Newcomers stumbled over many pitfalls and tended to resort to chemicals, or a mixture of vegetable and synthetic materials.

Though colour-fastness was a factor in the use of synthetic dyes, availability of the right plants was even more relevant. With the increase in the demand for cloth, many districts in the islands found themselves being denuded of suitable plants. Yet another factor which led to the use of synthetics was the need to extend the range of colours in the tweeds. Vegetable dyes, from the rather restricted range of plants available in the Hebrides, gave a limited variety of shades, and these were inevitably muted. With a market requiring variety, only synthetic dyes were able to satisfy the customers' demands for more and brighter shades.

First in the stage from sheep to wearer was the provision of the wool. By the early nineteenth century, the Blackface and Cheviot breeds had become well established in the Hebrides and the annual wool clip was steadily increasing. Each family had a few sheep which they sheared in July to use the wool for tweed, but if the family was a weaving one, much more wool was required than that from its own few sheep, and so supplies were bought from a merchant. The wool was first inspected closely to

79

remove all foreign matter, then thoroughly washed and dried. Afterwards it was teased and carded. The carding process took some considerable time and, with spinning, constituted a bottleneck to increased production. It was estimated that whereas preliminary processes took some 60 hours for a web of thirty yards (about 30 lb of wool), carding took 160 hours, spinning 240 hours, warping 2 hours, weaving about 60 hours and finishing 20 hours. One school favoured hand-carding, despite the drudgery it entailed, saying that machine-carding tended to injure the wool fibres, particularly the finer threads, and that the machine process took away some of the character of handwork. So far as the buyer was concerned, no great importance was attached to hand-carded tweeds; though these did find for themselves a market with those who fell in, either consciously or unconsciously, with the Ruskin school of thought. Hand-carded cloth also required a higher purchase price, which in itself tended to create a special market for it.

Spinning was of course a lighter task than hand-carding, demanding little except patience, the close attention of the spinner to the twist of the yarn, and the provision of a steady rhythm to the wheel. It was estimated, however, that this process took some 50 per cent of the total time taken to convert the wool to a web of finished cloth.

When machine processes for carding, and subsequently spinning, were introduced, many of the old school thought the thin edge of the wedge had been inserted : once one process had been mechanised, they argued, it would be only a matter of time before another and another would yield, until the hand-work element disappeared completely. There were also different opinions as to which processes might be better mechanised. Some went for hand-carding, but machine-spinning; others averred that machine-carding and hand-spinning was a much more acceptable sequence.

The carding mill erected at Tarbert in 1900 was not operated on a commercial basis but was intended by its builder, Sir

Samuel Scott, to be of benefit to the industry; if a net profit were made it would be applied for some public purpose in Harris. On the other hand, the two carding mills erected in Stornoway were commercial enterprises, intended to show a profit; they were the first ventures which proved that capital investment in plant to produce for a guaranteed market was much less of a risk than might—particularly in the Hebrides—be expected. While these 'capitalists' were businessmen they were also men of public spirit, and their actions laid the foundations for the present-day industry. The Tarbert carding mill depended on water-power for running the machinery and in 1911 work was suspended for six weeks owing to the very dry summer. Normally water is not available for a period of three weeks annually, and after 1911 further machinery was installed so that increased output would not be affected by future dry spells.

The provision of carding facilities gave rise to a number of anomalies. Stornoway was some 40 miles from Uig, on the west coast, and about 25 miles from Ness at the Butt of Lewis; thus the mills could not help all Lewis weavers equally. Again, weavers in North Uist and Benbecula had to send their wool the long, slow journey to Tarbert for carding. The charge for carding in Harris was 2d per lb; in Stornoway it was 3d per lb. So the Congested Districts Board was asked to erect small carding mills in the north and west of Lewis, and in North Uist. It was considered, however, that such plants would be using public funds to subsidise competition against existing private enterprises, and the requests were turned down. However, alternative suggestions were put forward, namely that the small carding mills required by isolated districts should be erected with capital provided either by a local businessman or by public subscription. It was pointed out that second-hand machinery was available at low prices; a teaser and carding machine could be bought for between £20 and £30. The building to house the machinery was hardly a problem, and the power required to drive the machinery was a nominal 6-7 bhp which could be produced either by water or by an engine. It was further suggested that facilities to provide the people with wool carded at cost price could be provided on a co-operative basis; but again nothing came of these projects.

In 1914, Professor W. R. Scott, who occupied the Adam Smith Chair of Political Economy at Glasgow University, presented his *Report to the Board of Agriculture for Scotland on Home Industries in the Highlands and Islands*. It contains much interesting material about craft industries and Harris Tweed in particular. The following is an appendix from the report on the earnings of labour in the making of various types of tweed :

'*1. Harris Tweed*

'The conditions under which Harris Tweed is produced involve that the worker purchases wool, and she has other outlays, such as the payment for carding (when, as is now usual, this is done at a mill), for weaving, and for other minor requisites. Accordingly, it is only after the deduction of these expenses from the price at which a piece of tweed is sold that the sum is reached which is earned by those who work at the dyeing, teasing, spinning, and finishing. The people generally work with units of 2 stones of wool, or 48 lbs. There is a considerable waste in the preliminary processes of washing and teasing. Thus the 48 lbs are reduced to 32 lbs when the wool is "Cross" or "Blackface". In Cheviot wool the loss is less, but the initial price is higher, and hence more tweed can be made from 2 stones of this wool. The "Cross" or "Blackface" wool is returned from carding weighing 30 lbs on an average.

'In the summer, especially if the weather is dry, the workers may have to wait for a considerable time for their carded wool, and allowance has to be made for the working hours thus lost. The longest process is that of hand-spinning. Many spinners say that, on an average, it takes a day to spin 1 lb of yarn—that for the warp takes longer, that for the woof less, and thus these workers could produce 3 lbs of warp yarn and 3 lbs of woof yarn in a week. Several good spinners regard this as slow working. One spoke of spinning 2 lbs of yarn in a day, but added that this would only occur under pressure, and that she could not accomplish as much the next day. Thus the spinning of the wool for a piece of Harris Tweed could be done in Harris in about thirty days or less. The working day is difficult to define. The women attend to their household duties in the morning, and begin to spin at 10 or 11 o'clock, working on till late at night. Most of them have a number of calls on their time, and hence it is more satisfactory to attempt to obtain a rough calculation as to the actual working hours, and to divide this into the sum available for the preliminary processes and spinning. Collating various estimates, the following result is obtained :

				£	s	d
44 yards of tweed sold at 3s net = 132s	...	...		6	12	0
Wool for 44 yards (2 stones) cost in 1911	£2	2	6d			
Carding 32 lbs at 2d per lb ...	...	£0	5	4d		
Soap, dyes (if purchased), sundries ...	£0	1	8d			
				2	9	6
Balance for hand labour				4	2	6
Weaving 40 hours, at 3d per yard, subject to allowance				0	11	6
Balance for labour, other than weaving				3	11	0

As to the time required for work other than weaving, Mr Malcolm MacKinnon, manager of the depot of the Scottish Home Industries Association at Tarbert, considers that an averagely good spinner would make 40 yards of tweed in 7 weeks, working 8 hours a day, ie in 336 hours working time, divided as to 80 hours for teasing, washing, and dyeing, and 256 hours for the spinning. Making a proportionate increase in the time, to provide for 44 yards instead of 40 yards, and adding an ample margin for time lost or for under-estimation, it may be taken that all the hand-work (save weaving) would not require more than 400 hours. This gives 2·125d per hour, so that the average worker can make over 10s per week; or, if she were skilful, requiring less time and obtaining more than the average for her tweed, she would earn proportionately more per week.

'There are two points which may be noted. When tweed sells at 3s per yard, that price is divided as below :

	s	d
Cost of hand-work in a yard of tweed	1	10½
Cost of materials and of carding for a yard of tweed	1	1½
	3	0

'In the second place, it sometimes happens that the workers use their own wool, or half the whole amount will be their own. On the basis of the difference between the buying and selling price of wool, according to the figures of the Scottish Home Industries Association, the amount such crofters would save by turning their wool into tweed would raise the value of the work to 2·3d per hour.

'A similar calculation made for Lewis resulted in very considerable divergence in the estimates, some placing the earnings per hour as low as a fraction over 1d, others at 1½d per hour. The following are the details :

Labour and Profit in Making Tweed

	A				B		
50 yards of tweed at 2s. 10d.		£7	1	8	at 2s. 9d. £6	17	6
2½ stones of wool at 23s.	£2 17 6			at 24s. £3	0	0	
Carding at 3d. per lb	0 12 0				0	11	0
Weaving at 3d. per yard subject to allowances	0 13 4				0	13	3
Soap (for washing wool) and soda					0	0	6
Dyes	0 8 0				0	2	6
Waulking expenses					0	2	6
		4	10	10	4	9	9
Balance for spinning, etc		£2	10	10	£2	7	9

84

TIME REQUIRED

Preliminary processes	...	...	...	60	hours	15	hours
Spinning	...	...	...	480	,,	396	,,
Finishing ...	...	...	...	32	,,	18	,,
Any other process ...	...	...	...	6	,,	—	,,
Total	...	...	...	578	,,	429	,,

'The comparative rarity of hand-spinning all the yarn for a web of cloth may account in part for the discrepancy in the estimates of the time required, though it should be added that the figures in Table B are furnished by the manager of the Crofters' Agency at Balallan, where good spinning is done. The chief point of interest, however, is the variation in the earnings per hour as compared with Harris. The chief causes of the variation are, first, that the Lewis hand-spun tweed is taken at 2s 9d or 2s 10 a yard, as compared with 3s net in Harris. Obviously, either spinning in Lewis is inferior, or else the prevalence of mill-spun yarn has drawn down the price of real Harris tweed made there, owing to the doubt as to its origin. In the second place, wool costs more, and a stone makes less tweed. Then carding is 50 per cent dearer, being 3d per lb, as against 2d per lb in Harris.

'In South Uist the conditions are different. There the people generally work their own wool, unless when the price is high, and then they sell it in the raw state. Few have enough wool to make a long web, and in this district the length of a piece is about 21 yards. The spinners work less persistently than in Harris, the time spent on spinning per day averaging four hours. Mr Gillies, manager for Mr Ferguson, merchant, Lochboisdale, gives the following estimates of cost of production and earnings:

	£ s d	
21 yards of tweed, sold at 2s 10d		2 19 6
Value of 26 lbs of wool £1 4 0		
Carding and carriage of wool to Tarbert 0 4 0		
Soap, etc 0 1 0		
		1 9 0

85

									s	d	
Balance in payment of labour	...	...	...	1	10	6
Weaving	...	...	...	...	...	...	0	7	0

Balance for hand labour, other than weaving ... 1 3 6

'The time required would be about 6 weeks, when 4 hours a day were worked on an average, so that the working hours would be between 140 and 150. This gives earnings of about 2d per hour, or rather less than in Harris, where the worker owns the wool.

'2.   *Tweed Made in Lewis of Machine-Spun Yarn*

'The usual price of mill-spun yarn, dyed, in 1911 was 1s 6d per lb. But 1 lb of yarn made more than 1 yard of tweed. A common quantity for yarn of average weight was 45 lbs of yarn to 50 yards of tweed. Hence the yarn in 1 yard of tweed costs 1s 5·2d. Weaving requires a trifle more than 3d for a yard of tweed, while finishing (waulking) and other work may be estimated at 1d per yard. Thus the cost of production will be as follows:

						s	d
Dyed yarn for 1 yard of tweed, at 1s 6d per lb	...	1	5·2
Weaving	...	...	...	...	...	...	0	3·18
Waulking, etc ...	...	...	...	...	...	0	1

1 9·38

'The cost of labour includes that of weaving, waulking, etc, and, in addition, the payments made to the workers in the factory where the wool is spun. It may be calculated that the cost of labour in producing 1 lb of dyed yarn is 1·25d. Therefore, on the basis of the average quantity of yarn in a yard of tweed, the latter figure is reduced to 1·125d. Adding these together, the total cost of labour (without allowing for profit) for a yard of tweed is almost 5·3d. The following are the details, the figures for Harris tweed, made in Harris, being added for comparison:

Cost of labour in the amount of dyed machine-spun yarn
required for 1 yard of tweed ...   .   1·125d
Weaving 1 yard of tweed   ...   .   3·18d
Waulking, etc   ...   .   1·00d

                                                      5·305d

Cost of hand-work in 1 yard of Harris Tweed made in Harris
is 22·5d.

'For a complete comparison something should be added to
the Harris figures to cover the cost of labour in carding.

'Finally, the cost of production of imitation Harris tweed,
manufactured by power-loom and of similar approximate width,
when wool is at the price given above, may be taken at 1s 6½d
per yard.

'3.   St Kilda Tweeds Carded by Hand

'With regard to St Kilda tweed, Mr A. G. Ferguson, 93 Hope
Street, Glasgow, calculates that a man and his wife working
together would make a web of St Kilda tweed of 30 yards in
5 weeks. The woman works 12 hours a day, that is, 360 hours,
while the man does all the weaving (which takes 48 hours), and
helps in the teasing and carding . . . the wool being valued at a
lower rate, being taken at only 9d per lb. Thus, the St Kilda
earnings would be approximately 1¾d per hour.'

YEARS OF CONSOLIDATION

The decision of the industry to form a body of association
and to apply for a standardisation mark (see page 123), was
implemented by the incorporation of the Harris Tweed Association in 1909 and the registration of its Orb mark which was
stamped on tweed hand-spun, hand-woven, dyed and finished
by hand in the Outer Hebrides. But this was far from being the
end of the industry's troubles and, in 1913, the price per yard

for tweed made in Lewis fell to 1s 9d and less; in May of that year it was stated that tweed hand-woven from machine-spun yarn was selling in London at 1s 6d per yard. One reason for this decline was the over-production of cloth during 1911 and 1912. The depression had its good effects, however, for it eliminated the very inferior tweeds, and many workers went over to using a well-dyed hand-spun weft with a machine-spun warp. It was being realised that with careful work, a hand-woven tweed with a characteristic colouring and design could be made from machine-spun yarn.

Fortunately at this time of decline, the industry was in the hands of producers who were able to insist on quality production. To their great credit, and to that of the weavers who rose to meet the new standards, this mill-spun cloth was of excellent quality. It was argued, and generally accepted, that healthy competition between this and the wholly hand-spun cloth would be of immense benefit to Lewis, provided that there was no misrepresentation on the part of the weavers who used mill-spun yarn.

However, even without deliberate misrepresentation, the name Harris Tweed was so deeply fixed in the minds of the public that it was impossible to eradicate it, despite the restriction of the Orb trade mark to wholly hand-spun cloths.

In 1913 a new tweed of the Harris type was introduced. This was a development encouraged by the Crofters' Agency, and was aimed at the makers-up of men's overcoats. The cloth was light yet warm, and contained more wool than the usual Harris Tweed, which required rather more than 1 lb of raw wool per yard. Workers received good prices for making it, and it proved to be a move in the right direction; indeed, it foreshadowed the efforts of the present-day industry to meet all the requirements of the market and to realise market potentials.

Then came the First World War. Among other aspects of island life, it seriously affected the tweed industry, particularly in Lewis where virtually all weaving was done by men; in Harris, as we have seen, weaving was still predominantly a female occupation.

Page 89: (above) Bales
of tweed packed for ex-
port; (below) applying
the Orb-mark stamp of
the Harris Tweed Associa-
tion.

Page 90: (above) Shipping bales of tweed on Stornoway's quay; (below) general view of Stornoway Harbour.

To fight the war, men had to leave their looms, and their places were taken with difficulty by women who had, in their turn, to leave their spinning-wheels. Thus, hand-spinning largely died out in Lewis. The war years were, in fact, a kind of hiatus in which the Harris Tweed Association became less of a force in the Harris Tweed industry, and the controversies between hand-spun and mill-spun producers lay dormant.

An incident in 1917 caused more than a little disquiet in the tweed industry. In that year the War Office introduced a compulsory-purchase scheme to prevent farmers from keeping wool to make garments for their own use. If the Order had been applied with full rigour in the Islands, the Harris Tweed industry would have died overnight, because it was then almost wholly dependent on local supplies of wool. Protest meetings were held, petitions were sent to the Scottish Secretary and the Secretary of State for War, and local ministers took up cudgels on behalf of their parishioners. Probably taken by surprise at the reaction of the islanders, the War Office claimed that the Order was all a misunderstanding and did not really apply to the Islands. Crofters were free to keep their own wool clip, and to buy additional wool to make tweed, the only condition imposed was that the extra wool had to be bought through a government-supervised depot.

After the armistice was signed, the tweed industry as a whole recommenced operations with the hope of expansion. The new era saw the Patent Slip Mill at Stornoway in the hands of fresh owners, Messrs S. A. Newall & Sons Ltd, who showed useful business acumen and who embarked on extensive advertising, as much on behalf of the industry as a whole as for themselves. Their entry into the industry is interesting. A Yorkshire farming family, they had come to Lewis in the nineteenth century to farm Aignish, some few miles east of Stornoway. Later they started a butchery business and, in the course of their dealings, began trading in tweeds for kind instead of cash. About 1906 their farm was taken over and carved up into crofts, so, concentrating their

F

interest in tweeds, they bought yarn and put it out for weaving. In 1918 they bought the Patent Slip Mill, with its carding and spinning equipment, and thus operated one of the two mills in Lewis, the other being that of Messrs K. MacKenzie Ltd on Lewis Street, Stornoway.

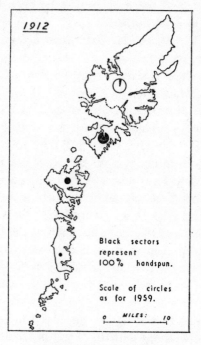

Output of tweed in 1912

The early 1920s were times for hard thinking, and particularly for considering the effects of the new practices appearing in Lewis. Harris was still faithfully producing the wholly hand-spun, hand-woven cloth which was eligible for the stamp of the Harris Tweed Association. In Lewis, on the other hand, events were running in a direction which, a decade later, was to lead to the revision of the definition of Harris Tweed.

A new figure who took an active interest in the production of

92

tweed, besides having many other activities to fill his agile business mind, now appeared on the island scene. This was Lord Leverhulme, who had bought the Lewis estate in 1917. Realising that progress in any industry was faster when only one pair of hands held the reins, he endeavoured to buy out the two Stornoway mills. He was able to come to terms with the MacKenzie mill but was unsuccessful with Newalls. The MacKenzie family retained an interest in their former firm, but Lord Leverhulme became the major shareholder and took over the running of the business. He also bought both North and South Harris, acquiring with the former the North Harris Carding Mill. The mill was run by the Lewis & Harris Handwoven Tweed Co, later the Harris Handwoven Tweed Co Ltd, and it was intended it should engage in commission spinning, though it also produced yarn on its own account. It was also proposed that the company should produce their own cloth. About 1923 Leverhulme started another carding and spinning mill at Geocrab in South Harris. This mill was also run by the Lewis & Harris Handwoven Tweed Co and was largely a philanthropic gesture to serve certain outlying Harris districts by carrying out machine carding and commission spinning. Thus by 1924 there were four spinning mills on the island.

Expansion of the tweed industry in Lewis was accentuated by another decline in the herring-fishing industry throwing many men on to the labour market. They turned to weaving, and this activity was further encouraged by local residents who acted as 'producers', buying yarn and putting it out for weaving. The Shawbost district on the west side of Lewis became particularly prominent, even outpacing the older centres of Lochs and Uig. Expansion of the industry in general was helped on by the introduction, encouraged by Lord Leverhulme, of the Hattersley domestic treadle loom, which was much quicker than the older wooden loom, and could weave more intricate patterns. From then on Hattersleys of Keighley maintained regular and direct contact with the Harris Tweed industry.

In the early postwar period, Leverhulme's influence led to a number of Hattersley looms being introduced into Kenneth MacKenzie's mill. This new departure seems to have been partly connected with the idea of training girls from the rural areas of the island in the craft of weaving. Leverhulme was inclined to favour complete mill production of tweed under a brand name, and certainly the commercial advantages to the mills of concentrating the weavers in the mill itself or in adjacent premises are obvious enough. This example was followed, though not on a large scale, by Newalls and also by some of the independent producers in Lewis. These 'independent producers' were those who, unlike the converters, had no spinning capacity of their own and who therefore obtained their yarn from either hand or machine spinners. The people working on looms installed on the producers' premises were an insignificant part of the total weaving force on the island; the vast majority of weavers worked at their own looms close to their croft houses. Where weavers did work in the mills, they were engaged as pattern-weavers or were under training. The practice of installing looms in mill or producer premises was short-lived and the 'home' feature of Harris Tweed never really departed from the traditional hand-weaving process.

The Leverhulme period also saw changes in other processes, in particular dyeing, spinning and finishing. It is true that a certain amount of dyeing on behalf of island producers had already taken place on the mainland in pre-1914 days, for instance in the case of coloured yarn supplied from some of the old Highland mills. But much of the wool spun on commission at that time on the mainland had been dyed by the crofters or producers in the islands, or else yarn imported from the mainland came to the islands in white hanks and was dyed locally—'in the yarn'. The Stornoway mills, being the largest producers of tweed with mill-spun yarn, were probably the first to carry out dyeing on the mainland to any significant degree as they had no real facilities of their own. Also they were already using mainland wool which had been blended and scoured for them as an additional service by the wool merchants. In any case, demands from the market for new colours and shades were virtually forcing the mills to look to the mainland, particularly the Borders area, for assistance. However, a large amount of home-dyed wool continued to be bought from the crofters, and in fact wool which had been imported from Scottish mainland sources was still sent out to the crofters for dyeing.

During the Leverhulme period, the use of island mill-spun yarn increased substantially, particularly in Lewis; the use of mainland mill-spun yarn also increased. Estimates indicate that during the 1920s the proportion of mainland mill-spun yarn to island mill-spun yarn never exceeded 50 per cent.

Finishing carried out by mainland firms for the large Lewis tweed producers was another result of Leverhulme's era of influence in Lewis. It is not clear at what time mainland finishing began to take place on a substantial scale, but again as the island's capacity for doing the work was limited, it was to be expected that the mills should turn to the expertise available on the mainland. It has been said that the mid-1920s saw the full use of mainland finishing of tweeds, but many of the small producers continued to rely on hand finishing until the mid-1930s and later.

To sum up, it was apparent that the Lewis side of the industry was expanding, and at a faster and steadier rate than the Harris side. This was evidenced by the comparatively small amounts of wholly hand-made Harris Tweed being stamped by the Harris Tweed Association between 1914 and 1933. In 1914, the figure was some 68,000 yards; thereafter came a decline, until the next peak figure of some 47,000 yards in 1920, and then a further decline until the lowest figure of 22,000 yards in 1933. The Lewis side was also becoming technically and commercially organised to a fairly high degree; and equally obviously, this growth into a mature full-scale industry was completely without the aid of the certification mark of the Harris Tweed Association. Indeed, the Association was in no real position to do anything except act as a

95

mere inspection and guaranteeing agency. Its stamping fee, originally ½d per yard, later increased to 1d per yard, brought insufficient revenue to enable it to do much to promote the interests of the wholly hand-spun side of the industry.

In 1925 Lord Leverhulme died and the whole running of the business of Kenneth MacKenzie Ltd was once more taken over by the original family. By this time the reputation of what was being called Harris Tweed, though it came from Lewis, had increased considerably, in fact to such an extent that new interest was aroused on the Scottish mainland, in England and in foreign countries. The tweed concerned was of good quality, with characteristics of its own and able to create its own market on its own merits; it virtually invited imitation and this, in fact, followed. Competitors in the textile field, on the Continent and even in Japan, began to produce cloth which was sold as Harris Tweed, quite unchallenged by the powerless Harris Tweed Association, and there was a very real possibility of the word 'Harris' becoming less of a description of origin and more an indication of a type of cloth. In fact by 1934 one authority on trade descriptions included Harris Tweed among a list of geographical terms which had come to denote types of commodities, like Eccles cakes. There is no doubt that had the name of Harris Tweed been further debased, any association of the cloth with the Hebrides would ultimately have been entirely lost, and the growing island industry, supplying such a large slice of the islands' economy, would have deteriorated in the face of competition which was better organised commercially and technically, and backed up by expertise not fully available in the Hebrides. Indeed, in 1933 a Japanese agent visited Lewis and unsuccessfully tried to obtain samples of the cloth and study the process of manufacture. The Lewis and Harris folk were as inscrutable as the Oriental gentleman himself; they gave nothing away.

In a way, the Lewis industry had created its own problems. First, it was itself using the term Harris Tweed to describe a product which did not wholly conform to the Harris Tweed

Association's definition; and it was relying to a certain extent on imported yarn from the mainland—in some instances the yarn was not even Scottish. This latter practice was common with the small producers of tweed who had no spinning facilities of their own; those who had their own mills were using exclusively island-spun yarn, though some of the wool was imported from the Scottish mainland. By the mid-1920s it is thought that the total output of Harris Tweed woven in the islands was about 500,000 yards, of which about 5 per cent was from mainland-spun yarn and some 35,000 yards was stamped by the Association as wholly hand-spun Harris Tweed. But it was the 5 per cent mainland-yarn element in the total tweed production which was the thin edge of the wedge and which invited such blatant competition and imitation from outsiders who had a keen eye to increased business and fat profits built on a reputation created by the island industry. Since mainland dyeing and finishing processes were used even by the mills, competitors quickly realised that they could sail close to the wind without let or hindrance. In 1927 one mainland competitor even went so far as to venture into the islands by setting up a shed beside the pier at Tarbert in Harris, and in it installing two wooden looms and two Hattersley looms. The system used was to send the firm's mainland-spun yarn to Harris, get the cloth woven at Tarbert into greasy or unfinished tweed, and have these webs returned to the mill on the mainland for finishing. Though the output was small it was a pointer to the lengths to which determined competitors would be prepared to go.

The intrusion did not of course go unnoticed. About 1930 another Scottish mainland firm, with experience of supplying yarn to weavers in the islands, moved into the production of tweed on their own account. Again the wool was spun at their mill, the yarn shipped to Stornoway, the greasy webs returned to their mill for finishing and the product marketed as Harris Tweed. Within four years their production had increased to some 50,000 yards per annum.

While the infiltration was going on, the Stornoway mills were increasing their production of yarn and also of finished tweed. Additions were made to their spindle capacity and a considerably increased proportion of the tweed hand-woven on commission for the mills in the Outer Hebrides began to be sent to the mainland for finishing. The reason for this move, in which the independent producers were participating to a greater extent than before, was the increasing demand by the 'bunch' trade for repeats of patterns and for a more uniform finish. Large multiple tailors were also demanding an ever-increasing supply of tweed for their shops. Though at this time a substantial amount of hand-finishing was being done in Lewis, it was not only insufficient to meet the demand, but, being a hand process, it did not always meet the standard required by wholesale buyers.

In 1930 the firm of James MacDonald Ltd were established, installed spinning machinery and finishing plant, and by 1933 were ready for business. The setting up of this finishing plant was significant, for it showed how the industry was eventually to shape, with all processes being done in the islands.

THE NEED FOR LEGISLATION

By the year 1934 there were an astonishing number of cloths on the market masquerading as 'Tweed', or 'Harris' or 'Harris Tweed'. These included Lewis Tweeds, Lewis Homespuns, Lewis and Harris Tweeds, Harris and Lewis Tweeds, Real Harris and Lewis Homespuns, Ceemo Tweeds (which were not in fact homespun), Aooo Harris Tweeds, Island Harris Tweeds, Handwoven Tweeds from the Islands of Harris and Lewis, Genuine Harris Handwoven (a power-loomed imitation), Llhanharris Tweed (possibly a Welsh connection here), Harris Style Tweeds, Harris Type Tweeds, Real Harris Tweeds, Imitation Harris Tweeds, and Imitation Harris Makes.

Such a plethora of cloths was more than disquieting and in the long run was bound to harm the island industry. There were seven broad groups of cloth reaching the final purchaser. These included:

1   Tweed hand-spun, hand-woven and hand-finished in the Outer Hebrides, both stamped and unstamped
2   The tweed which came to be called fifty-fifty tweed, which was often disposed of as hand-spun tweed although only the weft was hand-spun
3   Island-commissioned mill-spun tweed which was hand-finished in the islands
4   Mainland-commissioned mill-spun tweed which was hand-finished in the islands
5   Tweed hand-woven from both island and mainland yarns and hand-finished in the islands
6   Tweed hand-woven from both island and mainland yarns and finished in a mill on the mainland
7   Tweed power-loomed in the Borders, in Yorkshire and elsewhere

A substantial proportion of Nos 1, 2 and 3 was being made from island wool but some other cloths on the market could be described as rubbish, including one Harris Tweed which was 90 per cent cotton. Despite all these variations and imitations, the public generally still kept a picture of Harris Tweed being either wholly hand-made or at the very least having all its manufacturing processes carried out in the Outer Hebrides.

If the variety of fabrics was disquieting to the Lewis side of the industry, it was even more so to the producers of the wholly hand-made material. In 1928, the membership of the committee of management of the Harris Tweed Association changed and the new committee at once examined the way things were going. Although the Association was still pitifully small compared with the forces it intended to fight, it sensed that justice might be on its side. What it did know was that it had reached the point of no return; it had to move or become defunct. Through legal intermediaries it contacted the Lewis producers, particularly the mill-processing ones, and threatened legal action unless their cloth made from mill-spun yarn ceased to be described as genuine Harris Tweed. Though this threat was not entirely justifiable, the companies concerned were willing to face the challenge and took legal advice. This move was to prove significant for both parties and indeed for the Islanders as a whole : were it not for their tweed industry, they might have been by 1934 scattered throughout the world, beholding in dreams their native Hebrides under alien skies.

5 The Harris Tweed Association

FROM 1934 onwards the story of the Harris Tweed industry is largely the story of the Harris Tweed Association. But before dealing with the 1930s and subsequent decades, it is useful to review, in some detail, the history of the early days of the Association.

ASSOCIATION AND REGISTERED MARK

On 9 December 1909, the Harris Tweed Association was incorporated and started its career as watchdog for the growing industry. The main objects for which the company was established, as given in the memorandum of Company Articles of the Harris Tweed Association, were:

. . . the protection of the interests of manufacturers and merchants of and dealers in tweed made in the Islands of Harris, Lewis and Uist in Scotland, and to promote the manufacture and sale of such tweed. To protect the trade against offences under the Merchandise Marks Acts and otherwise to prevent the use of false trade marks and descriptions in respect of tweed made in imitation thereof. And in furtherance of such objects:

To register a trade mark or trade marks under the powers given by S.62 of the Trade Marks Act, 1905, and to use

101

such trade mark or trade marks and to register any such trade mark as a general trade mark or in respect to any specified goods or classes of goods as may be arranged or approved of by the Board of Trade. The Company to have complete control over the said trade mark and to permit such person or persons or incorporated body to use such trade mark on such conditions as if may think fit . . .

To print and publish any newspapers, periodicals, reports, books or leaflets that the Company may think desirable for the promotion of its objects . . .

To take any such legal proceedings as may be necessary or advisable from time to time against any person, persons or incorporated body which infringes or illegally uses the registered trade mark of this Company, and also so to do against any person, persons, or incorporated body which wrongly describes goods manufactured or sold by them or gives false inaccurate guarantees with regard to same . . .

To do all such other things as are incidental and conducive to the attainment of the above objects . . .

The first committee of management of the Association numbered six ie two nominees of the Crofters' Agency; two of the Scottish Home Industries Association; and two of the merchants of Harris and other districts who dealt in wholly hand-spun tweed. Mrs Mary Stewart MacKenzie, who represented the Crofters' Agency, became the first chairman and each member of the company undertook to pay a sum not exceeding £5 in the event of the company being wound up. The original subscribers were Millicent, Duchess of Sutherland; Mr William Harrison, described as an agricultural engineer but in fact a director of James Buchanan Ltd, the whisky distillers; Mrs Mary Stewart MacKenzie; Mr George Favorke, secretary to Lady Seaforth; Mr E. C. Brown, a London chartered accountant; and Mr Norman MacLeod and Mr Donald Morrison, both merchants of Tarbert.

The Association's first act was to apply for a standardisation mark, and the application to the Board of Trade contained the following statements:

The Company has been formed by various persons and Associations interested in the welfare of the crofters of the Outer Hebrides who are engaged in the manufacture of Tweeds, and the sole object of the Association is to encourage and foster such industry by such steps as may be deemed expedient, and incidentally to prevent as far as possible the fraudulent substitution of machine made Tweeds as genuine Home Spun Tweed made by the crofters of the Outer Hebrides (which comprise the Islands of Harris, Lewis, and Uist), and which Tweed has long been called and recognised both by the trade and the public as 'Harris Tweed', the name 'Harris' being originally derived from the Parish of Harris in the Long Island, which forms part of the Outer Hebrides.

One of the objects of the Company as expressed in the Memorandum of Association is the obtaining of a Trade Mark under S.62 of the Trade Marks Act of 1905 for the purpose of application to genuine Harris Tweed to enable the trade and public to readily discriminate between the genuine Harris Tweed and imitation Tweed, it having long been a grievance of the crofters, and those interested in their behalf, that large quantities of machine made Tweed are constantly sold as genuine 'Harris Tweed', meaning thereby the Tweed made by the crofters in the Outer Hebrides.

The industry is a struggling Home industry producing Tweed of considerable merit, and the only practical manner in which the trade and public can be educated to discriminate between the genuine and the imitation 'Harris Tweed' is by the application of a standardising mark uniformly to all genuine Tweed, and the Association has consequently applied for registration of the mark which forms the subject

103

of the above numbered application, under such Rules and Regulations as the Board of Trade may direct, to genuine Harris Tweed, it being intended that the actual place of manufacture shall in every case be applied with the Trade Mark according to whether the Tweed is made in the Island of Lewis, in the Parish of Harris or in the Island of Uist.

In due course, the Association was described as 'an Association for the Protection of the Harris Tweed Industry' and registered as the proprietors of the Standardisation (Certification) Mark No 319214 in Class 34 (Schedule III) in respect of Harris Tweed. The mark consists of an Orb surmounted by a Maltese Cross with the words 'Harris Tweed' subjoined. (These symbols came from the arms of the Earl of Dunmore, in recognition of the part played by the Countess of Dunmore in the promotion of Harris Tweed.) The definition of the mark was that ' "Harris Tweed" means a Tweed, hand spun, hand woven, dyed and finished by hand in the Islands of Lewis, Harris, Uist, Barra and their several purtenances and all known as the Outer Hebrides'.

The Board of Trade regulations also decreed that the Harris Tweed trade mark was the absolute property, and under the sole control, of the Harris Tweed Association Ltd, and that it should not be applied by any person except under sanction of an agent duly appointed by the Association's committee of management.

The conditions for the use of the mark included the following :

Wherever the Harris Tweed Trade Mark is used there shall be added in legible characters to the Harris Tweed Trade Mark the words 'Made in Harris' or 'Made in Lewis' or 'Made in Uist' or 'Made in Barra' as the case may be. . . .

The Committee of Management of the Association may with the sanction of the Board of Trade from time to time alter these Regulations or make new Regulations wholly or in part in lieu thereof. The Board of Trade reserve to themselves the right to cancel the Mark at any future time if in their opinion it should appear advisable so to do and their decision upon this point shall be conclusive.

Thus the Harris Tweed trade mark was registered as a mark of origin and mode of manufacture and the Board of Trade judged it to be in the public interest to permit the Association to act for the industry. The previous applications for trade marks for tweed were withdrawn. These had been made by independent bodies whose interests were now embodied in the Harris Tweed Association. Mrs Stewart MacKenzie agreed that the Seagull mark, obtained by her in 1907, be altered by the deletion of the words 'Harris and Long Island' from her mark's description.

During the first quarter of 1912, when the Lewis side of the industry was feeling a cold wind of depression, some Stornoway merchants negotiated with the Association for the introduction of the trade mark in Lewis, on condition that they should have representation on the committee of management. On 3 May 1912, the committee passed a resolution, confirmed on 3 June, that the offer from the Lewis merchants be accepted, and the committee be increased by two members nominated by the Lewis Harris Tweed Association. For the transaction of business, other than the election of members, at least four members of the eight-man committee were to be present at each meeting, and these were to include a representative of each of the four interests.

The governing body of the Association continued unchanged into the late 1920s, stamping a declining yardage of tweed conforming to the 1909 definition. In 1932, by a resolution of the committee of management, it ceased to be a representative body and from then on recruited new members by co-option. There are now only eight members and co-option must be unanimous.

THE FIRST TWENTY YEARS

The Harris Tweed Association began stamping tweed with its trade mark in 1911 at three centres: Tarbert, Geocrab in south

Harris, and Uist. For each of these stamping districts an inspector was employed. The main outlay of the Association was for the salaries of these inspectors, to which minor expenses, such as travelling, subsistence and even die-stamps and stamping ink were added. In the first year of operation (1911) the Association in each of the three districts defrayed its own expenses out of the $\frac{1}{2}$d per yard it levied on tweed stamped with the Orb mark, besides leaving a sum towards general expenses which could not be allocated to any particular district. Altogether 125,318 yards were stamped, yielding £261 4s 2$\frac{1}{2}$d. What may be described as normal working expenses came to £243 6s 1d, leaving a balance of £17 18s 1$\frac{1}{2}$d. Statistics of production had to be obtained, in order to determine the charge to be made for affixing the mark, so investigation was made at each place at which a stamper or inspector was employed, merchants collaborating in providing tweed returns to build up the following picture of production for the years 1910 and 1911.

1   *Harris*. In 1910 it was estimated that the output of genuine hand-spun tweeds amounted to 4,015 pieces, each averaging 43 yards. Some tweed containing mill-spun yarn was also made, estimated at 100 pieces of 43 yards each. The hand-spun material sold at 3s per yard, the mill-spun tweed at 2s 9d per yard. The total production of wholly hand-spun tweed was 172,545 yards; mill-spun cloth accounted for 4,300 yards; and the total cash value of production was £25,842. In 1911 output of pieces increased, but not significantly, though the increase in the average length of a piece to 45 yards brought in more money. The 1911 production of wholly hand-spun tweed was some 180,000 yards; its value was £27,135. The yardage output of tweeds of mill-spun yarn remained virtually static.

2   *North Uist*. The estimated output of tweed from North Uist was submitted by the Association's inspector who applied the stamp. His figure included the output from North Uist's small satellite islands, and also a certain amount, about 11 per cent, of tweed which was not presented for stamping, this cloth using

106

Page 107 : (left) An old loom from St Kilda, the only one in existence; (right) the St Kilda loom showing some details.

Page 108: (above) Scoured fleeces on fencing drying in the open air at Ardhasaig, north Harris *c* 1920; (below) dyeing wool in a large iron pot in Lewis *c* 1920.

partly or wholly mill-spun yarn. The figure for genuine hand-spun tweed was 46,440 yards, retailing at 2s 10d per yard, with a total cash value of £6,579.

3 *South Uist*. The making of tweed had not been taken up as extensively in this island as in other northern parts of the Hebrides, and the yardage output was of small value to the island community. The island merchants calculated the 1911 output to be worth under £1,000. The price per yard paid to the workers varied from 2s 9d to 2s 10½d. On this basis the total output was 6,500 yards with a total cash value of £907.

From these three sources the total output during 1911 amounted to 233,840 yards with a total cash value of £34,621.

4 *Lewis*. Though a certain amount of wholly hand-spun tweed was made in Lewis, the quantity could not be ascertained with any accuracy. On the other hand it was estimated that the output of partly or wholly mill-spun tweed was 6,500 pieces averaging 55 yards each, for which the workers were paid between 2s 8d to 3s per yard, giving an output total of 357,500 yards worth some £50,000. The depot of the Crofters' Agency at Balallan, which accepted genuine homespun tweeds, said that in 1911 some £500 was paid over to weavers.

5 *St Kilda*. Most of the St Kilda tweeds reached their market through the ordinary trading agencies; only a very small proportion was sold through the Home Industries Associations. Around the 1880s, when increased navigation brought tourists by the score to St Kilda, there was a ready on-the-spot sale for cloth products. Often a whole winter's production was sold in advance. The lack of competition however depressed the original high standards of both quality and design, and the St Kilda tweed trade nearly came to grief. By 1899 the cloth made in St Kilda was almost unsaleable. With subsequent improvements in both quality and quantity, St Kilda tweeds once again took their place in the market and met an increasing demand. The fact that the cloth came from a far corner of the earth enabled a few extra pence to be placed on its price. The 1911 production of St Kilda

was estimated at 3,000 yards, valued at 3s to 3s 3d per yard, totalling some £470.

At the time that the Association began its stamping, it was being alleged that tweed containing mill-spun yarn was still being sold as Harris Tweed. In the first nine months of 1911, there was a boom in the industry, particularly in Lewis; then came a slump through over-production and inferior workmanship, and the Harris Tweed Association decided to take action against this inferior mill-spun cloth. In November 1911, a tailor called Roderick MacLeod was charged with selling as genuine Harris Tweed a cloth made from yarn mill-spun in the islands; the summons, however, was dismissed. This was an unexpected blow, just at a time when the Association was beginning to get the feel of its duties, deepening the depression and slow sales experienced by the Lewis tweed industry.

Early in 1913 it was decided to appoint an inspector for Lewis. But at the end of that year it turned out that this new departure had cost some £53, and brought in about £13; thus, the whole operation for 1912 had in fact been a loss. However, 1911 had been a good year, and overall the Association expected to show a reasonable credit balance, and to use this balance to further the interests of the wholly hand-spun tweed industry. History, as it turned out was unkind, and the Association remained almost inactive until the early 1930s when it became the strong force for good which the Harris Tweed industry has on its side today.

THE 1930s

As was seen in Chapter 4, by the early 1930s the Harris Tweed Association knew it must take up cudgels on behalf of the Harris Tweed producers and it seemed that a large-scale legal battle was about to begin. Preparations for the fray took the form of protracted discussions between the intermediaries of both parties, for a number of factors had to be jointly considered

SUMMARY OF THE ACCOUNTS OF THE HARRIS TWEED ASSOCIATION, LTD., FOR 1911 AND 1912

I. INCOME AND EXPENDITURE ACCOUNTS

EXPENSES.

	1911. £ s. d.	1912. £ s. d.
Tarbert—		
Inspector's salary	70 0 0	80 0 0
Other expenses	14 11 2	3 9 5
South Harris—		
Inspector's salary	32 5 3	50 0 0
Other expenses	4 8 1½	0 19 10½
Uist and Bernera—		
Inspector's salary and travelling expenses	46 17 6	77 12 1
Other expenses	8 0 8	1 13 8
Lewis—		
Inspector's salary		52 10 0
Other expenses		1 1 4
General Expenses—		
Secretary's salary	35 0 0	
Travelling and hotel expenses of secretary	8 1 2	8 2 0
Travelling and hotel expenses of inspector from Lewis		3 10 10
Audit fee		2 2 0
Advertising	23 4 7	
Postages, stationery, and office expenses	9 11 6	7 19 2
Sundries	1 6 1½	
Total expenses	243 6 1	
Balance (1911)	17 18 1½	
Total	261 4 2½	314 0 4½

RECEIPTS FOR MARKING TWEED.

	1911. £ s. d.	1912. £ s. d.	Yards Stamped. 1911.	1912.
Tarbert	152 17 8	129 6 4½	73,384	62,073
South Harris	55 17 0½	74 11 10½	26,809	35,805
Uist and Bernera	52 9 6	59 12 11	25,188	28,630
Lewis		13 7 10		6,428
Total		276 19 0		
Balance (1912)		37 1 4½		
Total	261 4 2½	314 0 4½	125,381	132,936

II. GENERAL BALANCE SHEET, 31ST DECEMBER 1912

Creditors for cash advanced—				
Scottish Home Industries Association		£67 14 5		
Crofters' Agency		67 14 5		
Harris Tweed Association of Tarbert		33 17 8		
		£169 6 6		

Cash at bank and in hand, stock of stationery and ink	£67 8 6		
Less sundry creditors	21 6 9	£46 1 9	
Preliminary expenses incurred in forming the Association, and costs of obtaining special trade mark		54 6 0	
Expenses of 'Harris Tweed Case' (1911)	£130 4 3		
Less damages from John Bull (Ltd.)	100 0 0	30 4 3	
Law cost in connection with alteration of the Articles of Association, etc		3 13 0	
Cost of registering trade mark in Canada		8 0 0	
Cost of registering trade mark in U.S.A.		7 18 3	
Excess of expenditure over income		19 3 3	
		£169 6 6	

before agreeing to a confrontation in the courts. For instance the Association knew it had failed, indeed had been financially unable, to do anything about the rise in the growth of the Lewis tweed industry. The difficulties of dealing with the situation as it then was were real. Prosecution under the Merchandise Act in England could very well come to grief before a magistrate, and in Scotland criminal proceedings depended on action being initiated and the prosecution conducted by the Crown. Observations made on trial precedents, which were relatively simple, though parallel in content, indicated that a Harris Tweed prosecution could well end in defeat. Even an action for 'passing-off' would have been a tremendous enterprise.

It was realised by the Association that it was too late in the day to do anything effective to preserve the term Harris Tweed solely for the product of the Harris hand-spun industry, as the greater bulk of the cloth produced in the islands came from mill-spun yarn; in fact, it was learned that both the MacKenzie and the Newall mills contemplated an application to the Board of Trade to have the Association's certification mark withdrawn as being no longer representative of the industry. The Association itself therefore decided to have the definition of its trade mark altered to permit the stamping of tweed which had been made from island mill-spun yarn. It was seen that this politic move would in fact strengthen the industry and its association with the Outer Hebrides. At the same time, the Association wanted assurance from the mills that they would make available to small independent producers of tweeds sufficient quantities of island-spun yarn for them to be able to have a fair share of the yardage of Harris Tweed to be stamped under the new definition. Agreement was eventually reached on both sides but not before various other interested parties had entered into the controversy. Meetings were held in townships throughout Lewis and Harris and the local paper, the *Stornoway Gazette*, carried correspondence and reportage about the matter. The recession in the industry in the islands in the early 1930s and the anxiety caused by severe falls in the prices paid for hand-woven tweed added feeling to the controversy.

One of those who took an active interest was the then Member of Parliament for the Western Isles, Mr T. B. Wilson Ramsay, who concerned himself mainly with bringing the views of the various and often conflicting interests to the notice of the Board of Trade, the Government department principally concerned. His letters to the Press, eg, his letter to the *Stornoway Gazette*, 16 March 1934, show that he, like some others, was well aware of the dangers to the island industry's future if drastic steps were not taken. Lord Fincastle, son of the then Earl of Dunmore and a direct descendant of the Lady Dunmore who many years before had done so much to encourage the island industry, was also concerned with the situation, as was the Rev Murdo MacRae, (a Free Church Minister) of Kinloch in Lewis. He asserted that both the importation of yarn from outside the islands and also mainland finishing ought to be stopped and, as champion of the rural weavers, he found himself in conflict with the Stornoway mills. But once a formula satisfactory to the weavers had been found, Mr MacRae supported the alteration in the definition finally proposed—and in fact he became a member of the Harris Tweed Association and its committee of management.

By 1933 general agreement had been reached on a new definition for Harris Tweed. In particular, the interests in Harris who had been resolutely opposed to the admission of mill-spun yarn in any shape or form eventually accepted that mill-spun yarn might be admissable, provided that it was spun in the Outer Hebrides, thus ensuring that the tweed was, apart from imported virgin Scottish wool, an entirely island product.

It was partly to satisfy this group that the amended trade-mark regulations provided for tweeds made entirely from hand-spun yarn to have the word 'Handspun' added. To cater for geographical variations of Harris Tweed, provision was made, as before, for the cloth to be additionally stamped, along with the orb-and-cross mark, with the words 'Woven in Lewis',

113

'Woven in Harris', etc. Thus, the customer was protected against imitations.

On 23 June 1933, the Secretary of the Harris Tweed Association wrote a preliminary letter to an official of the Patent Office Trade Marks Branch with regard to the proposed amendments to the regulations and the definition to be contained therein; formal application was made on 30 June 1933. A question was raised as to whether tweed woven on Hattersley looms could properly be described as hand-woven; this was soon resolved, as the loom was operated by foot and the weaving process required the close attention and physical participation of the weaver.

Finally in 1934 the new definition appeared :

> 'Harris Tweed' means a Tweed made from pure virgin wool produced in Scotland, spun, dyed, and finished in the Outer Hebrides and handwoven by the Islanders at their own homes in the Islands of Lewis, Harris, Uist, Barra and their several purtenances and all known as the Outer Hebrides.

The words 'at their own homes' were designed to ensure that the hand-weaving remained a home or cottage industry and to prevent any concentration of weavers in mills or factories, a development which would have been contrary to the whole image of Harris Tweed. The word 'Islanders' was preferred to 'crofters', because the latter word was thought to have too limited a significance, though crofters were in fact the majority of the weaving population.

The introduction of the new definition resulted in some pronounced changes both within the island and outside. The mainland firm which in 1927 had set up its weaving shed in Tarbert for mainland-spun and mainland-finished cloth pulled out, bringing great relief throughout Lewis in particular. At last, it was said at the time, the Government had defined the material which in the future could alone be legitimately described and marketed as Harris Tweed. The position of the industry as a mainstay in the economy of the islands was also strengthened, particularly in Lewis, which stood to reap the greatest benefit. Without the 1934 legislation the island would undoubtedly have seen emigration on as large a scale as it had seen in the early 1920s. In addition, the increased amount of cloth available for the stamp (from 95,241 yards in 1934 to 1,485,246 yards in 1935) would increase the funds of the Harris Tweed Association, which could now put into effect its Articles of Association and properly serve the industry, both the wholly hand-spun side and the island mill-spun cloth producers. In fact the Association was able to embark on a world-wide advertising campaign on behalf of the new Harris Tweed industry, stressing that the raw material in the cloth was pure virgin wool produced in Scotland, and, by clear inference at least, disclosing that certain of the processes, namely, dyeing, spinning and finishing, although carried out in the Outer Hebrides, might be done by machinery.

So long as the main market for the cloth had been Britain, and production had been measured in, for the most part, tens of thousands of yards, the scope for competition from foreign sources was not great; indeed, the 1909 definition of Harris Tweed had tended to restrict commercial incursions to isolated instances. But with the introduction of the revised definition of the cloth in 1934, world interest began to centre on the Lewis sector of the industry. Simulations of the Orb trade mark began to appear, and the countless variations of both 'Harris' and 'Harris Tweed' led to customers accusing those parts of the industry which were not at fault of selling shoddy material, badly woven and with poor wearing qualities. The HTA's cloth labels, sewn on to finished garments, were forged in large numbers. Large-scale advertising to teach the public to recognise the genuine mark was realised to be the main line of defence, with legal action where the origin of a forgery could be traced.

In the islands, in direct consequence of the new definition, 1934 became a year of major organisation, some of it of a radical nature. It had at one time been contemplated that a dyeing,

115

spinning and finishing mill might be set up in the islands which would not itself produce or market tweed; the main object of this scheme was to satisfy the demands of the smaller tweed producers who, as already mentioned, felt that they were, or might be in the future, at a disadvantage in having to rely on the Stornoway mills, their largest competitors in the same market. The project had never come to anything. Instead, the two major tweed-producing concerns, MacKenzie and Newall, purchased their own dyeing and finishing plant. Another major firm, James MacDonald & Co Ltd, had already installed the full range of processing plant, which was in fact used by MacKenzie and Newall for a short time while their own was being installed. Towards the end of 1934 a new company, Messrs Thomas Smith & Co (Stornoway) Ltd, was started, building a mill to undertake spinning, carding, dyeing and finishing. By 1935 the islands had six spinning mills: four in Stornoway and two in Harris. In addition, Messrs Kemp & Co (Stornoway), set up by MacKenzies, offered an expert service in dyeing and finishing for those tweed producers who required it. There were, however, some small independent producers of tweed who still continued to use mainland mill-spun yarn and this led to a legal case of some interest.

THE EMBARGO CASE

The small independent producers had a minor share of the market, estimated at about 5 per cent. They sometimes bought island-spun yarn and became eligible for the stamp of the Harris Tweed Association; at other times they bought in yarn from the mainland and sold their cloth, by inference if not directly, as Harris Tweed. This activity was eventually brought to the attention of the Transport & General Workers' Union, which had always had an interest in the welfare of the Harris Tweed industry, since most of the weavers were its members, together with the great majority of those employed in the mills as spinners, warpers, and dyers; and, as it always supported the Harris Tweed

Association, it could hardly approve of producers who continued to use mainland yarn. As the dockers at Stornoway Harbour were also its members, it was seen that there was a weapon which could be used against the culprits : an embargo on the import of mainland yarn into the island.

In February 1938 the dockers refused to handle anything that resembled parcels or packages of mainland yarn, consigned to certain island firms, the chief of which was the Crofter Hand Woven Harris Tweed Co Ltd. The embargo was in operation for a short time only before it was lifted as the result of an Interim Interdict pronounced by the Court. The firm mentioned then brought an action against those officials of the Union who were apparently ringleaders in the dockers' action. This became known as the 'Embargo Case' and was heard first in the Scottish Court of Session and later in the House of Lords. It was eventually held that the predominant purpose of the combination between Trade Union officials and dockers was the legitimate promotion of the interests of the persons combining, and since the means employed were neither criminal nor tortuous in themselves, the combination was not unlawful. This case had a long line of precedents. Inevitably, Harris Tweed was brought into the case by the plaintiffs, later the appellants in the House of Lords. The investigation into the matter as set out in a House of Lords Report was the background for the Orb-mark litigation of 1963 (see Chapter 6) and was viewed by the industry with understandable concern.

The statement in the report which caused misgiving read :

> The description 'Harris Tweed' was originally applied to woollen cloth, which was not only woven by hand-looms in the cottages of the Outer Hebrides, but was so woven out of yarn spun by hand in the islands. Moreover, 'Harris Tweed' was hand-finished in the islands. It was thus a hand-produced and island-produced product throughout, and in 1911 a company limited by guarantee was registered under

117

the name of the Harris Tweed Association Ltd which
obtained a Trade Mark (referred to as the 'stamp') under
S.62 of the Trade Marks Act 1905, to apply to Harris
Tweed which satisfied those conditions.

After a time, the hand-spinning of wool into yarn ceased
to be commercially practicable and in 1934 the conditions
of the trade mark were varied, with the result that it could
apply to tweed hand-woven by the islanders in their own
homes out of yarn spun in island spinning-mills, and finished
in the island mills instead of by hand. Five such spinning
mills were established in Lewis. They did not use weaving
machinery, but by placing their yarn in the hands of the
hand-weaving crofters, cloth was produced which the mill-
owners, after 'finishing' it, could sell under the 'stamp'.
Ninety per cent of the spinners in the mills were members of
the Transport and General Workers' Union—the same trade
union as that to which all the Stornoway dockers belonged.
The percentage of trade-unionists among the weavers in
the cottages was much smaller. The officials of the union
desired that none but members of their union be employed,
but when this was asked of the mill-owners in 1935, together
with a rise in spinners' wages, the answer of the mills was
that this was in existing circumstances impossible, and that
a reduction in wages was more likely, owing (as was alleged)
to the cut-throat competition of independent producers of
cloth such as the appellants, who obtained their supplies of
yarn from the mainland at a cheaper price than that charged
by the mills.

This was satisfactory so far, but the statement went further:
'Cloth made out of mainland yarn could not carry the "stamp"
though it could be sold as "Harris Tweed" having been woven
in the island'.

The Harris Tweed Association took the view that Lord Simon's
statements of the facts, while no doubt accurately reflecting the

evidence given in the Court of first instance, did not settle once and for all whether for the purpose of the Merchandise Marks Act, the term Harris Tweed could lawfully be used to describe a tweed where the processes such as spinning, dyeing, and finishing, had not been carried out in the Outer Hebrides. On the other hand, the opponents of the Association maintained that Lord Simon's remarks were a charter for those wishing to use mainland-spun yarn. The House of Lords case was decided in 1941. Owing to the war conditions then prevailing, the Association confined its activities to advertising Harris Tweed and did not bring proceedings under the Merchandise Act mainly because of the great difficulties which would be involved, first in proving the use of mainland-spun yarn and then in getting together witnesses for its case.

WAR AND POSTWAR YEARS

During the years of the Second World War, production slumped from 4·0 million yards in 1940 to 1·7 million yards in 1943, with only a slight rise to 2·1 million yards in 1944. Most of the weavers had been called up for service in the armed forces. Also, with the exception of the Hebridean wool clip, wool rationing had come into force and remained thus throughout the war and for some years after. From 1942 onwards, industry in the islands came under the wartime Concentration of Industry Orders. This led to the closure for a considerable period of certain of the plants, including the dyeing and finishing plant of Messrs Thomas Smith, whose processing requirements were carried out by Messrs Kemp & Co. Substantial proportions of the spinning capacities of both the MacKenzie and Newall mills were also closed down.

When the war ended, an older generation remembered the speed with which arms were laid down and the tools of peace picked up again thirty years earlier. But now rationing and the restrictions of war lingered with the British public, relaxations arriving almost reluctantly, one by one. The output of Harris

119

Tweed increased at a satisfactory rate as returning servicemen took to their looms again, but the usual evils of rationing had become manifest in the islands, ranging from unhealthy scrambles for yarn to the appearance of the 'spiv'. Almost anything that remotely resembled Harris Tweed was put on the market and snapped up without too much enquiry as to its origin.

In particular, a method, used by small crofters who had gone into business on their own, and who were able to make substantial sales with a mere semblance of a marketing organisation, was to weave tweed very loosely in order to produce a greater yardage of cloth from a given quantity of yarn. To deal with this, the regulations for the certification mark of the Harris Tweed Association were amended on 19 June 1946, and the following condition was added: 'The Agents before affixing the Trade Mark to Tweed brought to them shall satisfy themselves that the same is entitled to be marked therewith and shall not afix the Trade Mark to any tweed which contains less than 18 picks and 18 ends per square inch of finished tweed'.

In the immediate postwar years, the Harris Tweed Association embarked on a national advertising campaign, as a means to create a lively marketing atmosphere for the cloth. To raise the increased revenue needed, on 1 January 1949 the stamping fee per yard of tweed was put up from 1d to 1½d; in 1955 it went up again to 2d per yard. In addition, the Association took its policing duties seriously and was able to take effective steps to prevent sales under the name Harris Tweed of cloth which had been made from mainland-spun yarn and, in some instances, finished on the mainland. The fact that the Association was now a real force able to extend significant pressure, and dedicated to safeguarding the product's future by preserving its unique character, was not lost on would-be imitators.

By the middle of the 1950s, vigilance and improvement in facilities had the industry soundly established. Many island producers duly went over to wholly island-spun yarn, but of course difficulties still arose, both within the islands and outside.

Important. — This Declaration Form must be signed by the owner of the tweed, and warning is given that any untrue statement in the Declaration will render the Declarant liable to severe penalties.

Piece No..............
Patt. No..............

I, ...

SOLEMNLY DECLARE that the Tweed Coloured ....

(of which a specimen piece is attached hereto) presented by me to be stamped with the Harris Tweed Trade Mark is made entirely from PURE VIRGIN WOOL PRODUCED IN SCOTLAND;

that the wool was DYED by ....

and .... SPUN by ....

and that the tweed has been HANDWOVEN by ....

.... at .... own home at..

Declared at .... the ....

day of .... 19 ....

Witness ....

Address ....

Occupation ....

Signature of Declarant } ....

Postal Address } ....

NOTE. — In the case of Tweed made from MILL-SPUN yarn the Suppliers' Invoice for the yarn must accompany this Declaration.

The Declaration Form of the Harris Tweed Association

A few small producers would mix island-spun with mainland-spun yarn, and present the resultant cloth for the Association's stamp. The inspectors were hard put to detect the deviation from genuine Harris Tweed, though by long and laborious methods the practice was stopped. Here the quantity of spurious cloth

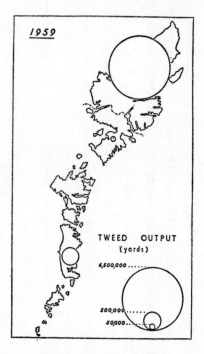

Tweed production in 1959

was negligible, but a more serious battle had to be fought with certain mainland firms who were selling as Harris Tweed, or with some name as near that as possible, a cloth woven but not otherwise manufactured in the Hebrides. Investigations proved that the annual yardage of this cloth was considerable and if allowed to continue its rate of growth could do untold damage to the island industry. The legal action which the Harris Tweed

Harris Tweed Association stamps

Association took against these manufacturers in 1963, and which is described in Chapter 6, proved to be the biggest task the Association had performed on behalf of the industry. The final judgment by Lord Hunter in July 1964, although it cleared away many of the would-be imitators from the scene, has by no means dried up the flow of tweed manufacturers who, in the opinion of the Association, are infringing the terms of the judgment and are sailing close to the wind.

THE ASSOCIATION TODAY

The Association employs a chief inspector at Stornoway and five full-time assistants. There are also five part-time inspectors to service Harris, including the islands of Scalpay and Bernera, and two part-time inspectors in the Uists.

A producer presenting tweed for stamping has to sign a declaration stating:

1 That the tweed is made entirely from pure virgin wool produced in Scotland
2 Where the wool was dyed
3 Where the wool was spun
4 By whom the tweed was handwoven

Where mill-spun yarn was used, the supplier's invoice has to be produced. The questions asked of course tie up with the 1934 definition.

Occasionally an inspector has his doubts about the genuineness of a tweed, and then calls upon the declarant to appear before a Justice of the Peace to make the declaration upon oath; past experience shows that this effectively discourages people from offering for stamping any cloth which does not conform to the specifications. It is now almost impossible for spurious cloth to be stamped.

Every quarter the spinners of yarn supply to the Association's

Page 125: (above) Old Lewis woman hand-carding wool *c* 1920; (below) old Lewis woman hand-spinning *c* 1920.

Page 126: (above) Lewis weaver at an old wooden beam loom *c* 1920; (below) group of Lewis women waulking a tweed *c* 1930.

chief inspector details of the quantities of yarn sold to individual producers. These are checked against the yardage stamped for each producer, so that any discrepancy can be detected and investigated. The producer who uses hand-spun yarn, and there are still a few, is entitled to have his cloth specially stamped.

The Harris Tweed Association has always been complimented on its achievement in making Harris Tweed so well-known throughout the world; but this has been done for the industry as a whole and not for any one large firm. It is essentially a passive mouthpiece for the industry and has no commitments to active work on the industry's behalf. Nor is it a trading company. Its Memorandum of Association sets limits on what it may do, since it has always to bear in mind that it is dealing with a number of firms who, within their own spheres, are highly competitive. As it holds information relating to production from competing interests, the Association does not publish accounts; to do so would be a breach of confidence. Its income now comes from the charge of 3d per yard for stamping with the Orb mark, and is spent on advertising, administration, public relations activities, mounting exhibitions, and legal fees in connection with registration of the mark in overseas countries.

The work of the Association has been described as a policing function for the tweed producers as a whole, and it is of course outside the islands, in a world which since the early days has been trying to cash in on the Outer Hebrides' staple industry, that its services are most needed. Tweed-producing firms who support it have representatives and agents in many countries who, apart from their commercial functions, act as on-the-spot detectives keeping alert for imitations of Harris Tweed. Occasionally check purchases of garments are made to obtain labels, which are then closely scrutinised for any variations from the Association's own. Often, as with forged banknotes, the spurious are difficult to distinguish from the genuine. In one instance a silk label was found which was an almost perfect imitation—except that the weave of the silk was in the wrong direction.

Once the source of a forged label has been discovered, and this often takes months of discreet enquiry, the Association places the matter in legal hands, and the source usually dries up completely. The Association has, through the years, taken the precaution of registering the Orb and Cross trade mark in over twenty foreign countries, including Canada and the USA, so that the mark has some legal standing there and it is easier to press home a charge of forgery or passing-off. Another aspect of the work of the Association is the prevention of the registration of marks or names too close to the Association's own mark or to the words Harris Tweed, particularly if these proposed marks or names are to be used in connection with textile products.

HARRIS TWEED PRODUCERS

Stephen Burns Ltd, Newton Street, Stornoway
R. Gillies & Son, Sandwick Road, Stornoway
Harris Handwoven Tweed Company Ltd, Tarbert, Harris
Harris Tweed Trading Company Ltd, Seaforth Road, Stornoway
A. MacAulay (Tweeds) Ltd, North Beach Street, Stornoway
James MacDonald Ltd, Seaforth Road, Stornoway
Kenneth MacKenzie Ltd, Sandwick Road, Stornoway
MacLean Tweed Company, Aignish, Isle of Lewis
MacLeod's Tweed Company Ltd, North Shawbost, Isle of Lewis
A. & A. MacLeod (Tweeds) Ltd, Marybank, Stornoway
John MacLeod & Company, New Shawbost, Stornoway
Kenneth MacLeod (Shawbost) Ltd, Shawbost, Isle of Lewis
S. A. Newall & Sons Ltd, James Street, Stornoway
Angus Nicolson, Inaclete Road, Stornoway
Seaforth Harris Tweeds Ltd, Caberfeidh Road, Stornoway
Lewis Smith, Balmerino Drive, Stornoway
Thomas Smith & Company (Stornoway) Ltd, Bells Road, Stornoway
D. Tolmie & Company Ltd, Francis Street, Stornoway

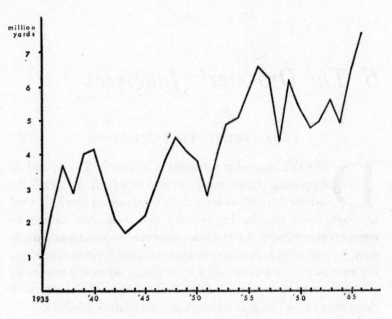

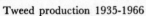

Tweed production 1935-1966

6 The Orb-mark Judgment

BACKGROUND TO LITIGATION

DESPITE the wide recognition of Harris Tweed and its supporting trade mark, firmly redefined in 1934, the industry's troubles with cloth marketed as Harris Tweed although using mainland-spun yarn and sometimes having no connection at all with the Hebrides were ever-recurring, as already seen. So long as the quantities of spurious cloth were insignificant, the encroachment was endured, except that when the sources of the cloth were discovered the Association raised the matter with those responsible; in many instances such sources dried up.

In 1946, however, a company was formed in Oban, on the mainland, named MacDonald's Tweeds Ltd. When the Harris Tweed Association wrote to the company about its selling tweed and offering to its customers labels reading 'Harris Tweed Guaranteed Hand Woven Made in Scotland', it stated that it had taken premises in Lochboisdale, South Uist, where its tweed was woven. The company claimed that its authority for doing so was the decision made by Lord Simon in the 'Embargo' case.

During the 1950s, the Harris Tweed Association was notified that an increasing and considerable amount of cloth appearing on the market as Harris Tweed was in fact not stamped with the

Orb mark. It was found that during 1953 some 750,000 yards of such tweed were produced; by 1955 the yardage had increased to $1\frac{1}{4}$ million. The Association decided to investigate and a senior inspector was sent to South Uist to find out what was really going on in the island. He discovered that the MacDonald's Lochboisdale weaving depot was a former tea-room converted into a small factory-type building in which fourteen looms were installed. At Eochar, some twenty miles north, the company had opened a larger depot where from fifty to sixty looms were installed in a hall and two sheds. On a rough estimate, there were some 120 looms at work producing tweed; others were distributed in weavers' homes throughout South Uist and Benbecula. In both the depots hand-weaving was being carried out in factory conditions. The weavers were treated as employed persons, though there was a certain elasticity about working hours and each weaver produced an average of two tweeds per week. The looms were supplied and maintained by the company, whose foremen tuned them and trained crofters in their operation.

Each piece of tweed produced was 42 yards long. Wages were 81s per piece plus a bonus of 7s if the weaver wove eight pieces in the month. The inspector found that the warps were power-warped in Oban and arrived in Lochboisdale beamed and ready for the loom. The weft was also filled on to bobbins in Oban, and the inspector considered the whole operation was a temporary undertaking just for the sake of having tweed woven in Uist.

Alarmed at the scale on which weaving was being done, the Association looked further into this activity which threatened to undermine not only its own work but also the whole economy of Harris and Lewis. The output of Uist-woven tweed was equivalent to some 17 per cent of the total output of tweed stamped by the Association, and it was increasing.

In 1952, a new company was formed, named Argyllshire Weavers Ltd, whose function was to market the tweed produced by MacDonald's of Oban. Also around 1952 two other mainland companies began to take an interest in the Harris Tweed market

131

and started operations reminiscent of pre-1934 days. It was obvious to the HTA that opposition of considerable proportions was building up. This opposition was finally named in 1958, with the registration of a company called the Independent Harris Tweed Producers Ltd, in which the interested parties were mainland concerns. Soon after its incorporation the company applied for a coat of arms with the intention of embodying in it devices or symbols which had some Harris significance. Objections were raised by the Harris Tweed Association :

It is believed and averred that the petitioners desire to obtain a grant of arms bearing an allusion to the history of Harris in order that they may bear and use such ensigns armorial commercially in trading for profit and that they thereby seek to encroach on the Islanders' industry by manufacturing a tweed called Harris Tweed, and yet, which does not comply with the accepted definition of the Harris Tweed. This would be to the severe prejudice of the respondents and those Islanders whose interest they represent.

The petitioners are a company who propose trading for profit in what they call Harris Tweed, their definition of which recites that it is 'cloth made from pure virgin wool dyed and spun in the Outer Hebrides or elsewhere in Scotland, hand-woven by the Islanders in the Outer Hebrides and finished in the Outer Hebrides or elsewhere in Scotland'. The wool thus used could be from any source whatsoever and much of the processing could, and it is believed would, be carried out on the mainland and not in the Islands. Processes such as dyeing, carding, spinning and finishing, which have traditionally always been carried on in the Islands and which are the costliest processes in producing the tweed, would it is believed be carried out on the mainland by the petitioners, none of whose members have a mill in the Outer Hebrides. The tweed they propose to trade in, thus, would not be genuine Harris Tweed and the use of arms connected with the Island of Harris would not in the circumstances be justified.

By the end of the 1950s it was decided that a move had to be made. Preparations were put in hand and legal action proposed. In 1960 there appeared in the courts the 'Spanish Champagne' case. In this, a French vineyard had gone to court against a Spanish firm because the latter had labelled its wine 'Champagne'. It was ruled that the Spanish label told a lie, as Champagne is in France. Though this case was less complex than the one in which the Harris Tweed industry was to become involved, it showed that the Association's case might win the day.

JUDGMENT FOR THE ORB MARK

The two parties in the action in the Scottish Court of Session were Argyllshire Weavers Ltd (and others) and A. MacAulay (Tweeds) Ltd (and others). First the action of passing-off raised the matter of Harris Tweed, the pursuers (Argyllshire Weavers) maintaining that it was a geographical name applying to goods : tweed handwoven in the Hebrides but with all other processes of manufacture permitted to be carried out on the mainland of Scotland. The question of whether or not the trade description of Harris Tweed was a proper one was also raised.

The pursuers were described as a group of Scottish tweed manufacturers who produced as Harris Tweed cloth which was handwoven in the Outer Hebrides but for which all other processes, such as spinning and finishing, were performed on the Scottish mainland. They raised the action against sixteen defenders, of whom fourteen were producers of Harris Tweed in the Outer Hebrides; one carried on business as a finisher for producers there, and the other was the Harris Tweed Association. The main aims of the action, brought in 1964, were :

1 To obtain a declaration that the pursuers were entitled to produce, process and market, in Scotland or elsewhere, as

Harris Tweed, cloth made from pure virgin wool produced in Scotland, dyed and spun in the Outer Hebrides or elsewhere in Scotland, handwoven by the Islanders in the Outer Hebrides and finished in the Outer Hebrides or elsewhere in Scotland.

2   To obtain an interdiction restraining the defenders from wrongfully asserting, in Scotland or elsewhere, that the cloth produced, processed, marketed and disposed of by the pursuers in Scotland or elsewhere as Harris Tweed was not Harris Tweed.

The defenders contended that it was essential for all processes to be carried out in the Outer Hebrides, as required in the definition of Harris Tweed laid down by the amended regulations of 1934 governing the use of the Harris Tweed trade mark, otherwise known as the Orb mark. They cited the 1909 Board of Trade definition of Harris Tweed as 'a tweed, handspun, handwoven, dyed and finished by hand in the Islands of Lewis, Harris, Uist, Barra and their several purtenances and all known as the Outer Hebrides'. At the outbreak of the First World War the reputation of the name Harris Tweed had been attached to the handmade tweed produced in its entirety in the Outer Hebrides. In the years following the war, although the purchasing public still thought of genuine Harris Tweed as the original hand-made product, substantial quantities of cloth spun, dyed and finished in mills on the mainland, sometimes from non-Scottish wools, were sold to the public as Harris Tweed. This led to the amended regulations of 1934 and to the public acceptance of three essential requirements for genuine Harris Tweed :

1   That it should be tweed made from pure virgin wool produced in Scotland.

2   That the handweaving should be carried out at the homes of the Islanders.

3   That the processes of dyeing, spinning, handweaving and finishing should be carried out in the Outer Hebrides.

It was held that the pursuers' action must fail, since the pro-

134

posed declaratory and interdict rulings, based as they were upon the definition of Harris Tweed promulgated by the Independent Harris Tweed Producers' Association, ignored the need for the tweed to be handwoven at the homes of the islanders and for the processes of dyeing, spinning and finishing to be carried out in the Outer Hebrides.

The pursuers contended that their claim for a declaration should be regarded as a 'passing-off action in reverse', so as to put upon the defenders the burden of showing that the trade description Harris Tweed, as applied to the pursuers' goods, was false. It was asserted that, by this standard, the claim could not be upheld.

Lord Hunter, before whom the case was presented, said that it was clear that those who produced tweed which qualified for the Orb mark, produced a tweed with the appearance, handling and wearing qualities which were recognised by the purchasing public as characteristic of Harris Tweed, and that to these qualities it owed part of its reputation. He said the pursuers had failed to prove that the cloth produced in accordance with their formula would necessarily have these well-known characteristics, or that it would necessarily even be tweed. He stated that the reputation of the genuine article with the purchasing public depended on its being handwoven tweed, wholly made, manufactured and produced in the Outer Hebrides from 100 per cent pure Scottish virgin wool. The name Harris Tweed had become distinctive of tweed made in this way.

Lord Hunter's judgment was the longest ever recorded in the history of the Scottish Court of Session, and ran to some 345 pages. In absolving the defenders from the action, which was for declarator and interdict, Lord Hunter said that the distinction between the definitions of the opposing parties, which raised the greatest controversy in the case, was as to the locality in which the processes of dyeing, spinning and finishing must be carried out to entitle the finished article to be sold as Harris Tweed. These processes, maintained the defenders, must be carried out in the

135

Outer Hebrides; while the pursuers maintained it was sufficient if they carried out the work 'somewhere in Scotland', ie either in the Outer Hebrides or on the mainland of Scotland.

Lord Hunter was far from being satisfied by some of the evidence presented—that the commercial reputation of Harris Tweed had been built on mainland yarn, still less on yarn mill-spun in Yorkshire. The converse was much nearer the truth; that mainland mill-spun yarn and sometimes Yorkshire mill-spun yarn were used in order to produce an imitation out of which quick and easy profits might be made under cover of the name and reputation of the genuine article.

One reason why Harris Tweed was purchased by the public, and also one of the reasons why producers and sellers of the cloth, including the pursuers, were so anxious to make use of the name, was its reputation as a home or cottage product. It was felt, and in his opinion rightly felt, by those who bought Harris Tweed, that they were assisting the inhabitants of remote islands to supplement the bare living they were able to wrest from the soil or from the sea by engaging in weaving in their own time, not necessarily inside the home, but in its reasonably close vicinity. The locality as much as, if not more than, the method of manufacture, had always formed an integral part of the reputation of Harris Tweed in the mind of the purchasing public.

Thus, finally, the island industry was supported by the law of Scotland.

7 The Industry Today

FROM WOOL TO YARN

ABOUT one-third of the Scottish wool clip goes into the Harris Tweed industry; much of the Hebridean wool clip is, by a curious anomaly, shipped to the mainland, as it is more suitable for carpeting than for clothing; it is estimated that the native clip is sufficient for only about three weeks' full-time production. There are some 2,000 Hebridean registered wool producers; the clip yields some 361,000 lb and is valued at about £73,000, wool being worth about 4s per lb. The island producers are given the choice of selling their wool for local manufacture or to the British Wool Marketing Board. All other producers in Scotland with more than four sheep are obliged to sell their wool to the board.

About 1·2 lb of raw wool from Cheviot and Scottish Blackface breeds is needed to make one yard of regulation Harris Tweed. Wool grows on the sheep in definite locks as distinct from the way in which hair grows, for example, on a cat. These locks are the staple, a word which has a long history in the woollen trade, and are made up of many thousands of individual fibres. The annual shearing in Scotland takes place in June or July, according to the weather. Shearers, necessarily expert in their work, use machine clippers to remove each fleece, which is then usually

137

folded lengthwise, with the shorn ends outwards. In the packing sheds the fleeces are packed into sheets for sending to the wool sorters. The fleece is placed on a table, its exterior upwards, and the sorter takes the various grades of staple from different parts of the fleece, throwing each kind into a separate basket; there may be up to six or eight grades of staple on a single fleece. The best quality, known as 'picklock', comes from the shoulder; a good fleece will yield a high proportion of this quality and therefore fetch a good price.

The wool is then baled and shipped to the Stornoway mills, where it is blended. Some consumers, particularly those in the USA, require soft blends; others require a harder blend, which means more Blackface than Cheviot. The UK market tends to favour a harder cloth. After blending, the wool is taken to be scoured or washed to remove impurities and make it white.

The dyeing process today, though conducted under mill conditions, requires as much skill, if not more, as was required in the early days when only years of experience and centuries of tradition guided the dyer. At present there are some 5,000 shades to choose from, including the old traditional crotal browns and heather colours, which are still in great demand by traditionalist purchasers. The subject of dyeing has its own extensive literature and is a science in its own right, requiring a knowledge of chemistry, light, colour, and the physical properties of the wool fibres.

During the scouring the wool fibres tend to 'felt' together, so they must be separated by teazing. This process includes the replacement of the natural oil removed in scouring, and also mixes the wool fibres according to the final cloth specification requirements.

The carding process, although now done by machine, has changed little from the very old days when hand cards were used. Large revolving cylinders covered with leather strips fitted with fine long wire teeth catch the wool fibres to straighten them out. In carding all the wool is used, and there is no removal of long

138

or short fibres. The wool is in fact carefully and methodically tangled, a quite different treatment from that given to the combed wool used for English worsted cloths, in which the fibres are disentangled. The carding process actually gives the final cloth its characteristic warmth, by incorporating far more air into its structure than is possible with combed fibres which lie smoothly against one another. The carded wool emerges from the machine in light strands called rovings and is wound into slivers or loose balls.

In the spinning process the carded wool is twisted into yarn. The machine here is the self-acting spinning mule, an elaboration of Hargreave's Spinning Jenny invented in 1764, and which was able to spin eight threads simultaneously. The spools of carded wool or slivers are laid on the delivery drums of the mule; each end is passed between rollers and given a turn round the spindles, which are on a moveable carriage. When the mule is set in motion, these spindles revolve, giving twist to the sliver, and at the same time the rollers deliver more sliver and the carriage moves away, keeping the yarn taut. When about two-thirds of the way out, the delivery rollers stop, but the carriage continues to the end of its two-yard travel and the yarn is reduced to its correct weight by stretch; the fibres, lubricated by oil, slip alongside one another until they are finally bound by the correct amount of twist. Should an uneven piece of sliver be twisted, the stretching will take place where the twist is least; ie at the thick part of the sliver, and will thin it down automatically to level the thread. In practice the less twist there is, the softer becomes the yarn; the more the twist, the greater the strength. After the twist has been completed, the carriage moves in again to the delivery rollers, winding up the spun yarn as it goes, and the whole process is repeated.

Warping is the next stage and is still a hand process, in which the warp threads are carefully built up according to the design of the pattern. Some designs are extremely complicated and the warper has to be a skilled worker. The warp is tied at intervals

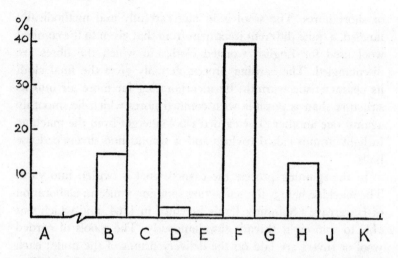

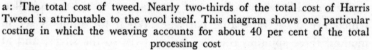

a: The total cost of tweed. Nearly two-thirds of the total cost of Harris Tweed is attributable to the wool itself. This diagram shows one particular costing in which the weaving accounts for about 40 per cent of the total processing cost

and put into bags for sending to the weaver together with sufficient weft yarn for the web. After the weaver has finished, the greasy web is collected by the mill or other tweed producer for finishing, inspection, checking and stamping with the Orb mark, and for dispatch to makers-up all over the world.

THE WORK OF THE WEAVER

The weavers of Harris Tweed, who provide the essential 'cottage' element in the manufacturing process, are self-employed. Many are crofters, and since the average size of croft is less than 20 acres, supporting perhaps only a cow and a few dozen sheep, they are really full-time weavers, dependent on the work for their livelihood, and part-time agriculturalists. Weaving can fit in with the seasonal and day-to-day requirements of the croft: planting, harvesting, peat-cutting, shearing, milking and the like. There is

140

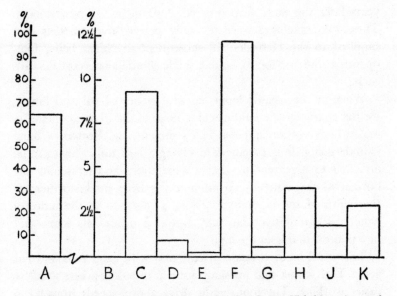

b: The cost of processes carried out in the Outer Hebrides. A, wool (delivered cost to Stornoway); B, dyeing; C, oiling, teazing, carding, spinning; D, warping; E, beaming; F, weaving; G, cartage to and from weaver; H, finishing; J, stamping; K, packing and carriage

no dictation from a factory hooter and the crofter-weaver can take up the hard and tedious work at the loom when he feels ready for it and when he cannot work outside.

The weavers own their looms, the majority of which are semi-automatic domestic-type Hattersleys with foot-operated treadles, the culmination of the long series of loom improvements which have evolved since the industry's early days. The first domestic loom of the type was made in 1894 and sold mostly to the Balkan countries, Turkey and Greece; it was usually made for a single shuttle. The first loom sent to Stornoway, a single-shuttle machine, was in response to an order placed in 1912 by the Lewis Mills Co Ltd, and was accompanied by a domestic weft winder; both machines were ordered for a power drive. The twelve-spindle winder cost £8 4s 9d with 7s 6d extra for the power drive. Two years later the same firm ordered a 90-in, 2×1 power loom. These two machines were the only power-driven models ever supplied to the Hebrides, all subsequent machines being foot-operated; the first foot-operated, single-shuttle looms cost £30 10s each.

Work at the treadle loom has always been hard and lonely, for the characteristic loud clacking noise of the loom in operation makes conversation impossible. At present, the Hattersley loom is undergoing design changes involving a new unit which can be attached to it, extending design capabilities and lightening the burden of the weaver. No attempt has been made to increase the width of the cloth from 29 in, as the cost to the industry would be prohibitive; not only would it mean new looms but new plant throughout the mills.

The usual loom is made of cast iron with cross rails and cut gears. Both crank and lowshaft are run in ball-bearings to allow easier working. The foot-treadle drive allows speeds from 80 to 140 picks per minute. Picking is by the overpick system, the pickers sliding on spindles. The checking is done by a spring-steel sweller in conjunction with a running check strap. Take-up is positive, the cloth being woven with absolute evenness over a wide range of picks per inch, without the use of changewheels. The 'Stornoway' take-up motion arrangement was made in order that larger-diameter rolls of cloth could be accommodated. Originally, when cotton and finer yarns were used on the looms a 12 in maximum roll was considered adequate; for the thicker Harris Tweed, however, a larger roll diameter of 16 in is needed. The present day loom costs about £130; a bobbin winder costs about £30. These two items are the main equipment which the weaver purchases and loans are often available. It has been estimated that some £250,000 has been invested in the Harris Tweed industry by individual crofters and this is another unusual aspect of the industry.

A finished tweed is 75 yd long and 29 in wide, and requires 70 lb of yarn, which in turn is the product of 100 lb of greasy

Page 143: (above) Stretching and rolling up a length of tweed c 1920; (below) Harris woman waulking a piece of hand-woven tweed in 1967.

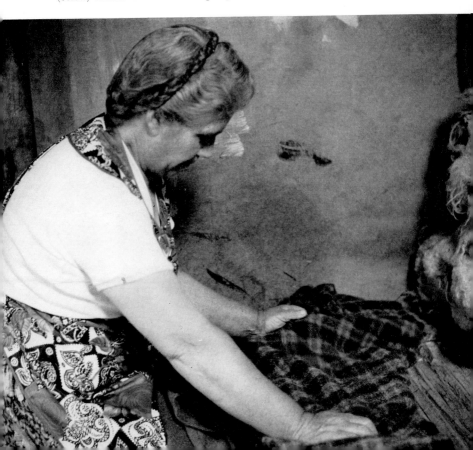

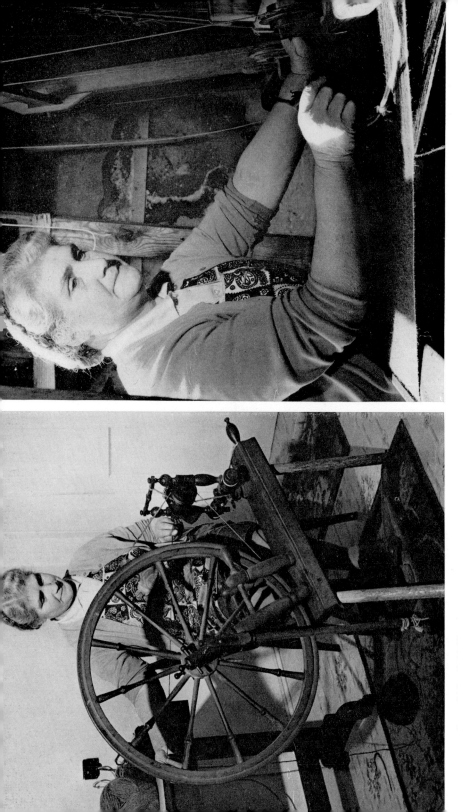

Page 144: (left) Harris woman hand-spinning wool in 1967; (right) Harris woman working an old wooden beam loom in 1967.

wool. The average web of unfinished, greasy tweed is about 80 yd long and $28\frac{1}{2}$ in wide (for two to six shuttles and a weft of eighteen shots per inch). The weaver can complete three tweeds a week when he is on virtually full-time weaving work with little or no attention paid to the croft; for these he will receive about £24. However, most weavers average $2\frac{1}{2}$ tweeds or less each week. If a design is intricate, or there are more colours than usual involved, the reward per web is higher. The money is paid out by a mobile bank which makes the round of the island's townships, saving the weaver the long journey to and from Stornoway to collect his money. The average annual earnings of weavers are £800-£1,000 per annum; those who can produce really first-class work and can cope with intricate designs, and who also deliver to a buyer's deadline, can earn more.

The weaver is in a rather strange position industrially, generally negotiating annual contracts with tweed producers who spin the yarn, warp it, supply it to the weavers and take back the woven cloth for final processing and dispatch. He usually belongs to the weavers' section of the Transport & General Workers' Union; yet for National Insurance purposes he is regarded as being self-employed. As such the weaver-crofter does not, in slack times or in times of trade recession, qualify for unemployment benefit and he also has to pay a higher rate of National Insurance contribution. At every General Election this grievance is aired by weavers who think that their anomalous position should be rectified. In 1966 a referendum was conducted by the TGWU to ascertain the feelings of the majority of them on this question, of which both sides were put to them. On the one hand they could agree to a contractual arrangement with a tweed producer, who would become their employer, and thus place themselves alongside other workers in industry, with regulated hours of work, overtime payments, holidays with pay, industrial injuries benefit and the other normalities of factory life. On the other hand, they could remain masters of their own time and with a degree of independence allowing them to attend to their crofts. Most weavers chose to retain what sometimes seems to them a doubtful freedom.

It is not an exaggeration to say that if it were not for the Harris Tweed industry the island of Harris-with-Lewis would be economically infertile. The industry is just about the only successful amalgamation of cottage industry and modern factory in today's industrial milieu. It is also an industry which is admirably suited to the economic survival of the area in which it exists. Because it is cash-producing, it has provided the means whereby crofters have been able to improve their standards of living. Both the town of Stornoway and the countryside of Lewis and Harris have benefited, though of course the town has stood to gain more since the industry is largely concentrated within its boundaries.

The Harris Tweed industry, however, based as it is on the island crofting community, is dispersed over a wide area, thus it is not efficient in the economic sense of the term. But social responsibility has prevailed over the knowledge that more concentration and more mechanisation of the weaving aspect of the industry would lead to greater economic returns.

The present output per annum is around 7,000,000 yards, though this figure varies according to demand and market changes. Of this output, at least two-thirds is exported, much of it to the USA. This outstanding achievement in the export field by a cottage-based industry in the remote Hebrides was recognised by an award from the export magazine *Ambassador*, as was Scotland's other famous export, whisky.

The mills on the islands employ about 1,000 people, an infinitesimal proportion of the numbers in the British textile industry as a whole. There are some 1,500 active weavers in the islands, most of them employed on commission weaving for the mills or the smaller tweed producers. If this weaving force is added to the mill-worker figure, the Hebridean proportion of the workers in the British employment category of woollen and worsted manufacturing and finishing is still only a fraction of 1 per cent. Yet though the numbers are so small, they are socially and economically highly significant for the islands, ever haunted by an unemployment figure of around 30 per cent; 20 per cent of those employed work in the textile industry.

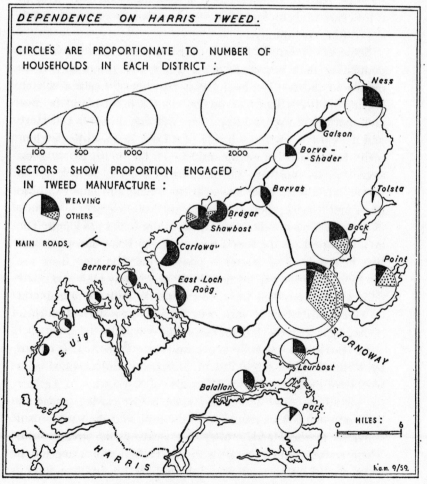

Economic dependence on Harris Tweed

147

Besides the Stornoway mills, there is a small mill concentration in Shawbost, on the west side of Lewis, belonging to Messrs Kenneth MacLeod (Shawbost) Ltd. This business started in 1915 in a small way, in 1935 became a limited company, and in 1960 added a finishing plant. In 1966 a further extension made the mill a comparatively large industrial complex for one of the remotest parts of Britain. The mill dyes the wool, cards it, spins it into yarn and employs some seventy people from the surrounding crofting community.

Some Lewis districts have of course more weavers per head of population than others. Before 1920, weaving was carried on mainly in the two southern Lewis parishes of Lochs and Uig. During the 1920s Shawbost, on the west side of the island, became an important centre, and from there weaving spread to Carloway and the various townships beside East Loch Roag. Little development took place before the middle of the 1940s in the Ness district at the northern tip of Lewis. Here the outlook of the people has always been seawards, to fishing and latterly to the Merchant Service; there is a significant Norse element in the folk of Ness. However, today every township in Lewis has looms. The area with perhaps the fewest weavers is the Point district, on the Eye Peninsula. The reason is possibly that the men there are mostly in full-time employment in the Stornoway mills and travel daily to and from their work. In general the mills try to maintain an even distribution of yarn over the island to weavers on their books; some weavers work for more than one mill.

In Harris, the one fully active mill is at Tarbert. It is owned by Kenneth MacKenzie Ltd of Stornoway and supplied with wool dyed by Messrs Kemp & Co, also of Stornoway. At Tarbert the already scoured and mixed wool is first carded, and then spun on one of three machines in the mill, and the yarn is then delivered to the Harris crofters for weaving into greasy webs. These crofters return the webs to the Tarbert mill, whence it is transported back to Stornoway for finishing. The mill employs a manager and staff of over twenty and at times shift work is necessary to keep pace with demand. Some of the weavers employed are in Tarbert, others are scattered throughout Harris. The mill built by Lord Leverhulme at Geocrab in 1923 was closed when the industry experienced a slump in the 1950s and is now used as a store. The Highland Home Industries Ltd, an echo from the old association days at the turn of this century, employs Harris weavers who, in 1965, produced some 3,500 yards of tweed. These weavers for the most part produce their own wool which they dye—often by the traditional methods—before sending it away to be carded. On its return, it is spun into warp and weft, ready for weaving. Very few original hand-looms, probably only about five, now remain on the island, but at Leverburgh and Drinishader there are two frames reckoned to be over a century old, thus providing a tangible link between the industry of today and its very humble beginnings. The tweed output of North and South Uist has not in recent years been substantial. The output of the spinning mill at Loch Eport in North Uist has been taken mainly by the Lewis producers. South Uist has the best land in the islands for crofting and, in addition, a prosperous seaweed industry.

OLD SKILLS DECLINE

Wholly hand-spun cloth was still produced in Harris during the years following the Second World War. Spinning wheels were in regular use, as were a number of the old wooden looms. Most of the webs were by then finished in Stornoway, though some were finished by hand. Inevitably the cost of production of the wholly hand-spun cloth was greater than that of mill-spun tweed which was also mill-finished. The hand-looms were slower, and the range of patterns available was restricted; whilst a unique cloth could be produced, it had to command a fairly high price. Some weavers went over to a fifty-fifty cloth in which only the warp was mill-spun, while the weft was hand-spun. In 1947, to help the Harris weavers, who had never really shared in the Lewis boom, a special cachet was brought into use to indicate

149

the use of hand-spun weft in the cloth. It was discontinued in 1956, though in 1960 the matter was raised again by the Harris District Council. However, as the Stornoway mills were reluctant to continue carding for hand-spinners in view of the small quantities involved and therefore the high machine cost, hand-spinning in Harris virtually went out of existence. This trend was further accentuated by the fact that though a number of women could still spin for weft yarn, there were very few who could spin good warp yarn. So the spinning wheel was almost completely abandoned in Harris, as it had been in Lewis some thirty years earlier. At the end of the war, Harris had about 200 looms at work compared with the Lewis figure of about 1,000 but the imposition of a crippling rate of purchase tax and other marketing difficulties discouraged many Harris weavers.

Producers, in the Lewis sense, were never a feature of the Harris part of the industry; nor were the Stornoway mills and non-mill producers so keen to send their yarn some 40 to 50 miles south for weaving when there were Lewis weavers nearer to hand. The organisation of motor transport for collecting greasy webs from the weavers was another aspect which resulted in the Harris weavers never really participating to a significant degree in the Lewis side of the industry. Harris weaving has always lacked an essential element of organisation. Only a fraction of Harris men work as full-time weavers for Stornoway producers; and these are nearly all on the boundary of Harris-with-Lewis, and have their own transport, so that a quick return of greasy webs for the yarn supplied is assured. The custom of spare-time weaving by women is not conducive to the rapid and regular return of webs which manufacturers must have if orders are to be completed promptly.

A certain amount of hand-spinning, hand-weaving and hand-finishing still goes on, with vegetable dyeing of mill-carded wool. But this output is small, though it does have its own special market composed of people who value the inherent qualities of wholly hand-made cloth and are willing to pay for what they want. These customers are often individuals who have come into contact either with weavers or makers while on holiday in Harris. The cloth costs up to three times that of the general run of tweed. A few Harris families still continue the age-old tradition of using their own wool clip to produce their own cloth; these carry on the last traces of a true domestic activity. In 1952 output of tweed from Harris was about 20,000 yards compared with some 4,000,000 yards in Lewis. Although in recent years the yardage output per annum has increased slightly, by far the main source of Harris Tweed is Lewis and it is mill-spun.

The demand for the wholly hand-woven cloth is high and, because only the Outer Hebrides can supply the genuine article, the potential is great. Unfortunately, the average age of the traditional weavers is increasing and the skill could ultimately die with them. Though there have been attempts to train others, particularly young people, the results so far are not sufficient to guarantee the continuity of the craft on a significantly commercial scale.

Waulking is still done by hand, a few women getting together for a shrinking session. It may be accompanied by a few songs, but the process is not now the social event it used to be.

IN THE FASHION

The growth of the Harris Tweed industry has been a mixture of good fortune and good business methods; the latter in particular have enabled it to withstand the assaults of really big commercial competitors. Despite the flooding of markets with man-made fibres, Harris Tweed has not only managed to hold its own but to improve its position and to meet the challenges of the times—while still retaining the essential qualities of a superior tweed, rugged in appearance, almost waterproof, warm in winter, and cool in summer. These qualities, married to new techniques, give the all-wool cloth a head-start in the textile markets of the world.

That the fame of Harris Tweed travels to remote corners of the earth is endorsed by the great fund of anecdotes about it. For instance, during the last war, a Lascar was being refitted in a Merchant Navy Comforts Centre in Glasgow after being shipwrecked. He was offered suit after suit, but, muttering 'Utility' he refused them all until, almost at the end of the line of clothes he saw an old Harris Tweed jacket. He picked it up, sniffed it and a broad grin split his face: 'That good. Me like smell of heather.' Another story concerns a photographer in Korea during the Korean War, who having had a reasonable fill of battle pictures was looking around for the unusual. He came across a young Korean boy playing at soldiers wearing an ill-fitting battle-dress as a uniform. The 'flash', however, was none other than an Orb-mark label issued by the Harris Tweed Association.

D. MacLure wrote in the *Spectator* of meeting the tweed in unexpected guise.

I have never seen anyone quite so dirty and disreputable. The would-be (Indian) fortune-teller stood shuffling his feet in the sand. A sickly grin demonstrated to perfection a set of fangs in the very last stages of decay. A greasy black fez hid the top of his head, and a ragged red-stained beard exempted him from washing the lower part. His dhoti was in shreds and heavy with the dust of centuries; yet he was wearing a Harris Tweed sports jacket that I myself would have been loath to part with. True, it was a little shabby and had already collected a modicum of uncleanliness, but at least the seams were holding together, and the cut of the coat still struggled to retain its dignity. The history of that coat, I thought, if ever truthfully told might prove rather interesting.

Just after the last war, a soldier from Stornoway was on a mopping-up operation in a remote area of the Malayan Peninsula. In one native village the first sight which caught his eye was a weathered, sun-faded sign-board above what had once been a shop. It read not only 'D. MacLeod, Merchant' (a typical enough Lewis surname), but also 'Harris Tweeds Sold Here'.

Similarly, the manager of a Stornoway tweed firm was on holiday in Egypt, paid a visit to the pyramids—and found a yellowed copy of one of his own firm's advertisements lying in the sand.

The author once found himself in an army camp scheduled to have a regulation hair-cut from a talkative Italian barber who snapped his scissors and, in the course of conversation, asked where his victim came from. On hearing that it was Stornoway, he immediately complained that he had a Harris Tweed overcoat which had once been his father's; he dearly wanted a change, but felt it would be wasteful to buy another coat until the tweed one had become worn out: and when would that be . . . ?

A recent survey made on behalf of the industry by the Harris Tweed Association underlined his words. The Italians stated that this hard-wearing quality was why they bought Harris Tweed, as did the Canadians, Dutch, Austrians, French and Belgians. The Finns, however, thought its attractions lay in its look and feel. Other countries picked out the fact of its being hand-woven; Danes described it as fashionable, and West Germans mentioned its 'snob appeal'. All acknowledged that the Orb mark of the HTA had contributed to its export success.

From its early days in the sporting-gentry market, the cloth now receives the attention of top fashion designers. Ted Lapidus, Jean Muir, Mary Quant, Sybil Zelker of Polly Peck, Ossie Clark of Quorum, Sally Foale and Marion Tuffin, Marion McDonnell and Susan Small, have all used it, recognising its endless varieties of checks, stripes, two-tones, pastels and subtle traditional hues. The early cloth was essentially masculine; durable, heavy, hairy, with rather dour colours and a limited range of weaves. Today, while still retaining its traditional qualities it has made a startling breakaway from long-standing patterns, colours, weights and functions. It has also proved a success as an upholstery material. Guy Rogers was the first firm to apply Harris Tweed in this way, teaming it with afrormosia wood for a range of modern furniture. At a recent Scottish Motor Show, Mercedes Benz showed an elegant convertible with Harris Tweed upholstery. The cloth has also been used for slippers and house footwear, for curtain materials and as a floor covering.

Its everyday uses remain, of course, for sports coats, top coats and suits for men, for suits, coats and skirts for women—and, in a lightweight cloth, even for evening dresses. The weights available range from standard (11 oz) to lightweight (8-9 oz) and bantam-weight (6-7 oz).

List of Dates

c 1372   Traditional date of the introduction of the Cheviot sheep to Scotland

c 1580   Documentary evidence showing weaving to be an activity of economic significance to Lewis and Harris

1760   Introduction of Blackface sheep to Highlands

1791   Introduction of Cheviot sheep to Highlands

1846   First web of tweed sold by the 'Paisley Sisters' of Strond, in Harris

1877   Making of South Uist Tweed for sale in London

1881   First Lewis Tweed sold

1888   Depot for Harris Tweed and knitwear in London opened by Mrs Thomas

1889   Scottish Home Industries Association founded

1889   Highland Home Industries & Arts Association founded

1896   Scottish Home Industries Association incorporated

1896   Crofters' Agency established

1897   Congested Districts Board came into being

1900   Carding mill erected at Tarbert in Harris

1902   Visit to Stornoway of King Edward VII and Queen Alexandra

1903   Carding mill erected in Stornoway

1905   Trade Marks Act

1906   Erection of carding and spinning mill in Stornoway

1906   Henry Lyons of London convicted of selling imitation Harris Tweed

155

List of Dates

1907   First web of tweed woven in Ness sold

1907   Seagull trade mark registered for Harris Tweed for the Crofters' Agency

1909   Harris Tweed Association founded, with Orb mark

1911   Stamping of wholly hand-spun Harris Tweed began

1911   Further carding plant added to Tarbert mill

1911   Harris Tweed Association's unsuccessful charge of fraud against tailor Roderick MacLeod

1912   Stornoway merchants joined Harris Tweed Association

1913   The Scott Report to the Board of Agriculture for Scotland on *Home Industries in the Highlands and Islands*

1917   Lewis bought by Lord Leverhulme

1923   Carding mill erected at Geocrab in Harris

1927   Mainland spinner began production of tweed in Tarbert

1933   Application to Board of Trade by Harris Tweed Association for new definition to include island mill-spun yarn

1934   New definition for Harris Tweed

1964   Judgment by Lord Hunter in favour of Harris Tweed definition of 1934

Gaelic Terms used in Cloth-making

(The English pronunciation given in brackets)

Achfhuinn mhiadhoin
(Ackinn Viain)

A word from South Uist. Part of the spinning wheel. It was the bar on which rested the two uprights which held the bobbin

Aireamh
(Ahroo)

A term connected with weaving, while setting the yarn for the loom. Iron pegs were driven into the earthen floor in two rows, the distance of a yard-stick from each other. The yarn was wound round these from side to side. Then the threads were counted in hundreds, each hundred tied together with a coloured thread. The odd number over a hundred was called *aireamh*, eg, *coig cheud is ceathair ar fhichead air aireamh* means 524 odd

Alt
(Ahlt)

The grain seen in cloth coming straight from the loom. This grain is seen until the waulking process makes the cloth homogeneous

Armadh
(Arumugh)

Grease added to the wool while it is being carded

Beairt
(Byarst)

The loom

Gaelic Terms used in Cloth-making

Beairt-fhighe (Byarst-Eeugh)	Weaving frame (the loom)
Beairtich (Byarstich)	To put thread on the loom
Caisreagan (Cashrugan)	The entangling of threads in warping
Calanas (Kalanas)	Wool working, from the raw material to the finished cloth
Caoibean (Koo-e-bun)	The 5 or 6 in of warp uncrossed by the weft at the beginning of the web
Casachan (Kasachan)	The pedals of a weaving loom
Cleith-luaidh (Kleea-looai)	The fulling- or waulking-frame
Clisnean (Klishnun)	The name given to each of the two pins fixed into the ground in warping thread. One was fixed at the end of each row of pegs, one about a foot from off the left-hand corner, and the other the same from the near right-hand corner
Cnagan (Cnagun)	A pulley in a weaving loom
Coinneal corn (Kanyul korn)	Rolling up cloth into a web
Corn (Korn)	Web of cloth
Crann (Krahoon)	The machine on which a thing is designed, such as *crann-deilbh*—the upright frame on which the *inneach*, or weft, was laid
Crois-iarna (Krosh-eearnah)	The simple frame, composed of a central piece, to either end of which a cross-piece was attached, like the letter T, but with their planes at right angles to each other. The *iarna*, or hank, was formed on this as it was unwound off the reel of the spinning wheel

Cromadh (Kromagh)	A measurement, equal to about 4½ in (the length of the middle finger over its three joints)
Cuigeal agus fearsaid (Kooig-al agus fyarshatch)	Distaff and spindle
Dealg (Jahlag)	The pin in a shuttle bobbin
Deilbh (Jayluv)	Framing witchcrafts by crossing different coloured threads in various ways as is done when threads are arranged for the loom
Disnean (Jeesnan)	Warping pins
Dluth (Dloo)	The warp
Earasaid (Yarusatch)	A wide mantle formerly worn by Highland women. Occasionally it was made from tartan, but generally from heavy cloth
Faiogh (Foo-e)	Thigging or genteel begging. In the Middle Ages it was common practice in Britain to obtain wool for a web of cloth by begging. In 1414 the Scottish Parliament passed an Act against 'thiggers' and 'sorners', these being the social pests of the period
Fuidheag (Fooyag)	Thrum; the warp-thread, 10-12 in long, remaining unwoven at the end of the web
Garman (Garaman)	Weaver's beam
Inneach (Innyuch)	The weft
Iteachan (Itch-a-chan)	The bobbin inside the shuttle

159

Gaelic Terms used in Cloth-making

Liodan an fhucadair (Leedan un ookadar)	Teasel *(Dipsacus fullonum)*, 'Fuller's Teasel', so called because it was used to raise the nap on woollen cloth by means of the strong hooked scales upon its spherical calyxes
Liosradh (Lyeaserugh)	Process of polishing fine woollen cloth and stamping flowers on it by passing through hot plates
Mudag (Moodag)	A little wickerwork creel completely closed in, except for one small opening at the side to admit the hand; used for holding teased wool
Olainn (Olin)	Wool
Seol-coise (Shawul-kosha)	The foot-board or pedal of the spinning-wheel

Bibliography

The following bibliography includes works in which there is only a passing reference to cloth-making. They have been mentioned because they give useful background information on the general economic and social conditions, past and present, of the Highlands and Islands.

Andersson, O. On Gaelic Folk Music from the Isle of Lewis. The *Budklaven*, No 1-4, Sect 3, 1952

Beveridge, E. *North Uist*. London, 1911

Bolton, E. M. *Lichens for Vegetable Dyeing*. London, 1960

British Wool Marketing Board. *British Sheep Breeds—their wool and its uses*. London, 1967

Buchan, A. *A Description of St Kilda*. Edinburgh, 1727

Bücher, K. *Arbeit und Rhytmus*. Berlin, 1897

Burt, E. *Letters from a Gentleman in the North of Scotland*. 2 Vols. London, 1754

Campbell, J. L. *Highland Songs of the Forty-five*. Edinburgh, 1933

Campbell, J. L. *Gaelic Words and Expressions from South Uist and Eriskay*. Dublin, 1958

Campbell, J. L. *Gaelic Folk-songs from the Isle of Barra* (booklet with records—Parlophone). London, 1950

Campbell, J. L. and Collinson, F. *Hebridean Folk-songs*. The MacCormick Collection of Waulking Songs, London, 1968

Campbell, M. S. *The Flora of Uig*. Arbroath, 1945

Carmichael, A. *Carmina Gadelica*. Vols I, II, 1928; Vol III, 1940; Vol IV, 1941; Vol V, 1954 Edinburgh

Bibliography

Comunn nam Fhion Ghael. *Leabhar Comunn nam Fhion Ghael.* London, 1886

Congested District Board. *Annual Reports.* Edinburgh, 1899-1911

Connell, R. *St Kilda and the St Kildans.* London, 1887

Craig, K. C. *Orain Luaidh Mairi Nighean Alasdair.* Glasgow, 1949

Crofters Commission Committee. *Report on the Social Condition of the People of Lewis in 1901 compared with Twenty Years Ago.* Edinburgh, 1902

Crofters Commission. *Annual Reports.* Inverness, in progress

Cumming, C. F. Gordon. *In the Hebrides.* London, 1886

Darling F. Fraser. *West Highland Survey.* London, 1955

Edinburgh College of Art, School of Town & Country Planning. *Harris 1966*

Ferguson, T. *Scottish Social Welfare.* London, 1959

Firth, J. *Reminiscences of an Orkney Parish.* Stromness, 1922

Geddes, A. *The Isle of Lewis and Harris.* Edinburgh, 1955

Geikie, A. *The Scenery of Scotland.* London, 1887

Goodrich-Freer, A. *The Outer Isles.* London, 1902

Henshall, A. S. 'Early Textiles found in Scotland'. *Proceedings, Society of Antiquaries of Scotland,* Vol LXXXVIII, 1956

Highlands & Islands Development Board. *Annual Reports.* Inverness, in progress

Highland Village Association Limited. *Home Life of the Highlanders, 1400-1746.* Glasgow, 1911

Hooper, L. *Weaving with Small Appliances.* London, 1922-5

Kennedy Fraser, M. *Songs of the Hebrides,* Vol I, 1909; Vol II, 1917; Vol III, 1921; Vol IV, 1925

Lewis Association. *Report No 2.* Stornoway, 1945

Lightfoot, J. *Flora Scotica.* 2 Vols. London, 1777

MacFadyen, J. *Sgeulaiche nan Caol.* Glasgow, 1902

MacFarlane, M. *Studies in Gaelic Music. Trans* Gaelic Soc Inverness, Vol XXVII, 1908-11

MacFarlane, M. *Gaelic Names of Plants: Study of their Uses and Lore. Trans* Gaelic Soc Inverness, Vol XXXII, 1924-5

McIan, —. *Highlanders at Home.* Glasgow, 1900

MacIver, D. 'Tweed Weaving'. *A Guide to Stornoway,* 1912

MacKeller, Mary. *The Waulking Day, with Songs.* Trans Gaelic Soc Inverness, Vol XIII, 1887

Morrison, N. 'Vegetable Dyeing in Lewis'. *Scottish Field,* June 1929

Munro, D. *Description of the Western Isles of Scotland, called the Hebrides.* Glasgow, 1884

National Association of Scottish Woollen Manufacturers. *Scottish Woollens.* Edinburgh, 1956

New Statistical Account of Scotland. Edinburgh, 1845

Old Statistical Account of Scotland. Edinburgh, 1794

Pennant, T. *A Tour in Scotland and Voyage in the Outer Hebrides.* London, 1772

Rainnie, G. F. *The Woollen and Worsted Industry.* London, 1965

Ross, J. 'A Classification of Gaelic Folk-song'. *Scottish Studies,* Vol I, No 1, 1957

Ross, J. 'The Sub-literary Tradition in Scottish Gaelic Song-poetry'. *Eigse, a Journal of Irish Studies,* Vols VII and VIII, 1952-5

Ruskin, John. *Lectures on Art,* 1890

Ruskin, John. 'The Seven Lamps of Architecture'. *Works,* 1907

Sands, J. *Out of the World, or Life in St Kilda.* London, 1888

Scott, W. R. *Report to the Board of Agriculture on Home Industries in the Highlands and Islands.* (Parliamentary Paper.) Edinburgh, 1914

Scottish Council on Industry. *Report of the Committee on the Crofter Woollen Industry.* Edinburgh, 1946

Scottish Country Industries Development Trust. *Annual Reports.* Edinburgh, in progress

Scottish Economic Committee. *Report on the Highlands and Islands.* Edinburgh, 1938

Scottish Home Industries. Book privately printed, c 1885

Shaw, M. F. *Folksongs and Folklore of South Uist.* London, 1955

Smith, P. G. A. *The Romance of Harris.* Edinburgh, 1914

Smith, W. A. *Lewisiana.* Paisley, 1886

Sobieski, J. and Stuart, C. E. *Lays of the Deer Forest.* London, 1848

Society of Antiquaries of Scotland. *Proceedings,* Vol LXVIII, 1934; Vol LXIX, 1935; Vol LXXI, 1937

Thompson, F. G. *Folklore Elements in 'Carmina Gadelica'.* Trans Gaelic Soc Inverness, Vol XLIV, 1964-6

Bibliography

Thompson, F. G. *Harris and Lewis.* Newton Abbot, 1968

Thomson, J. and MacDonald, D. *Orain Leodhais.* Stornoway, 1938

Tolmie, F. *Tolmie Collection of Gaelic Folksongs. Journal* English Folk Song Society, Vol IV, 1916

Walker, J. *Economical History of the Hebrides.* London, 1808

White, T. A. Blanco (ed). Reports of Patent, Design and Trade Mark Cases. No 16. *Argyllshire Weavers Ltd v MacAulay, A. (Tweeds) Ltd. (Trade Description, Trade Libel).* London, 1964

Working Party Report. *Wool.* HMSO, 1947

Acknowledgments

The author acknowledges with sincere thanks the help of many who gave assistance in one way or another in the collection of material for this book. In particular the following must be singled out: Miss Marion Campbell, Plocropol, Miss Mary Ross, Geocrab, and John Morrison, Northton, all of Harris; I. R. MacKay, Inverness, who took the trouble to uncover some early references to cloth-making; Dr H. A. Moisley, Dept of Geography, University of Reading; J. G. Jeffs, Kircudbright; W. H. Renfrew, Secretary of the Harris Tweed Association; members of the Harris Tweed industry in Stornoway who advised me on technical details; Messrs George Hattersley & Sons Ltd, Keighley; and librarians up and down the country who supplied useful bibliographical references.

I have also to acknowledge permission readily and freely granted to reproduce material from works by John Lorne Campbell of Canna; Mrs J. L. Campbell (Margaret Fay Shaw) of Canna; the Trustees of *Carmina Gadelica* (Oliver & Boyd, Edinburgh).

Lastly I would like to thank my wife, Margaret, who provided most of the line drawings.

Appendix

FOLKLORE and WAULKING SONGS

FOLKLORE

Long before Harris Tweed became Harris or even Tweed, the thick, heavy characteristic cloth made in the Highlands and Islands was known as *clo mor*, the big cloth, to distinguish it from that other cloth, tartan, which was more directly associated with the Highlands. While the *clo mor* was purely functional, in the intemperate climate of the west, the tartan had other uses than as mere clothing material. It had, for instance, a designatory function, distinguishing the member of one clan from another— useful in inter-clan battles. The result was that the tartan was given more prominence in Gaelic song and literature than the more humble *clo mor*. However, the *clo mor* has in fact won the day, for it has been the means through which a vast store of Gaelic song tradition has been preserved with a fidelity which no other medium could offer. This tradition is embodied in the waulking songs, whose extent is unique in the world.

The various processes in making the cloth, shearing, washing, dyeing, carding, spinning, weaving and waulking, attracted elements of folklore from other activities in the domestic life of the Gael. Plants, for instance, were more associated with healing properties than with dyeing. For healing to be effective, certain acts had to be performed, which acts brought in a religio-magical element to guarantee the efficacy of the proposed cure.

The most beautiful dye of all was once procured from a kind of rue. This plant has golden blossoms and grows on sandy shores, or machars; its long tough roots when powdered and boiled produced an excellent red dye. The plant was, however, more valuable for binding the sand: when it was uprooted the hole left tended to accelerate the erosion of the sandy soil, so it was regarded as a crime to pick it. There is a tale of one woman in the islands who longed to dye her cloth a rich red colour. She knew of this plant and went by dark of night to gather it, in defiance of her husband's prohibition. All through that night he waited for his wife's return, but as each slow hour passed there was neither sight nor sound of her. Then, at the darkest hour before the dawn, the northern sky was suddenly lit up with a glaring red light, and flashing colours were seen such as had never been seen before. When the Islanders heard of the missing woman they declared that surely had her spirit good cause to rue that red dye.

While the cloth was being waulked, and songs were sung to help along the work, it was necessary to ensure that the same song was not used twice at the same waulking; if it were, the cloth would become thin and streaky, and as white as the fleece of the sheep which had provided the wool. And as for the singer, there was no telling what might happen to her, nor indeed to the intended wearer of the cloth.

The effect of what was called the 'evil eye' was feared for all domestic activities, including cloth-making. The fairies, those aloof inhabitants of the half-world between this and the next, were prevented from damaging the web of cloth over a Sunday by the placing of two coloured threads on the loom in the form of a cross, and if the threads were red, then they were believed to be all the more effective. If cloth was made for a sailor or fisherman, great care had to be taken to ensure that the dye used was not derived from the crotal, the lichen which was gathered from rocks. To the fisherman, who had his own peculiar occupational superstitions, the association this plant had with rocks was enough to guarantee the wrecking of his boat. Strangely, the black crotal is said to have a water-proofing effect on wool—a property presumably seldom tested by fishermen.

The number of stages in the waulking process has some significance—seven, if two sub-stages are included. This was one of the magic numbers for the Gael, as indeed were three, five and nine. In some districts there were nine or twelve stages; all these numbers had Biblical associations or were echoes of tales from Celtic mythology. Many of the supernatural beings which figure in Gaelic folklore are founded on pagan animistic beliefs. Each household activity, performed either within the four walls of the house or as an extra-mural task within the confines of the croft, would have its associated spirit : the *gruagach*, for example, was a fairy woman who looked after the herding of cattle. The various phases of cloth-making were presided over by the *loireag*, a woman of indeterminate nature and description who was said to sit in at every waulking. Libations of milk were sometimes made to her, poured on to a special rock set aside for the purpose to ensure that the waulking in particular went well and without hindrance, and indeed with her blessing.

While the obvious inference to be drawn from much of the folklore associated with domestic activities is that it was based on rank superstition, analysis of many of the associated songs, chants, and utterances indicates elements more properly termed religious than superstitious. As in other stores of folklore in Highland and other societies, evidence points to a gradual, imperceptible assimilation of natural observations into a body which originally comprised magical and supernatural elements; a sustained, developed accretion from the time when Christianity had not yet been born, and animism, often associated with the Druidic forms of religion, was the only regular and organised medium available through which people could express themselves spiritually.

Thursday was always regarded as being an auspicious day on

which to begin cloth-making operations. Thursday was the day of St Columba, a Celtic saint with head-and-shoulders standing above all those others of the old Celtic Church who endeavoured to introduce Christian doctrines to the early Gaels. Thus his favour was invoked for each task in cloth-making, just as Biblical and other Celtic saints were invoked, with utterances of a religious and secular nature, when other specific tasks were begun.

WAULKING SONGS

Waulking, the fulling, shrinking or thickening of the cloth when taken from the weaver's loom and handed over for final processing, was a communal process performed, in the Hebrides, exclusively by groups of women, who made it an event of social significance. As we have seen, the process is known in other parts of Europe, as is its performance to the rhythmic accompaniment of song; but nowhere does the song culture associated with waulking have such richness and wide variation as in Gaelic Scotland.

A waulking song, unlike many other labour or work songs, hardly ever makes reference to the waulking process in its theme. Even incidental textual allusions to it are rare. The term waulking song merely implies that it has been used in that occupation. On the other hand, rowing songs, milking songs, herding songs, spinning songs nearly always contain some reference to function. The origin of the songs described as waulking songs is often obscure, and it is a reasonable assumption that most of them were not originally composed for use within the waulking group, but were adapted by the waulking women for the purpose. The thematic content of the songs is wide, possibly indicating that they were in fact borrowings either from a literary tradition, from the compositions of poets (though not necessarily bards within the precise definition of the term), or from songs composed from personal experience within the mainstream of Highland life: laments, other labour songs, love songs, eulogies and the like.

The waulking song is recognised by its hard definite rhythm matching the physical rhythms of the work, and by the definite vocal punctuations, generally in the form of a chorus of syllables. To fit in with the rigid rhythmic requirements of the waulking, a song not originally intended for the purpose often had to be wrenched from its normal accentuations, with sometimes no regard to the continuity or logic of the original theme. Also, lines would be interrupted by the choral repetition of abstract syllabic refrains. These refrains have mnemonic significance, so that the chorus could be sung correctly, led by a soloist who sang the lines of the song which told the tale, to give at least a semblance of continuity.

A song used for waulking had often to be extended to fit the time needed for the process. In the words of the Gaelic scholar, the late Rev Kenneth MacLeod, who collaborated with M. Kennedy Fraser in collecting Hebridean songs: 'In the Hebrides labour and song went hand in hand; labour gave rise to song and song lightened the labour . . . Cloth for Sunday wear gets about two hours' waulking; cloth for the wear and tear of tilling and boating has to be thicker, and gets at least double the time. No one ever asks, however, "How long will it take?" but "How many songs will it take?" ' To lengthen them, many songs were sung in lines, or half lines, interrupted by the chorus. There are many structural variations among the waulking songs in existence today; half-line verse and chorus; one-line verse and chorus; one-line verse and three-line chorus; two-line couplets and three-line chorus, etc.

On occasion songs were composed specifically for the waulking group. Though not falling into any particular textual type, they generally praised the cloth and the waulking women. Poets like Alexander MacDonald tended to use the medium to convey strong political allusions, eg Jacobite prejudices. In some stages of the waulking process, songs were composed within the waulking circle itself, in which allusions were made to the work, or else were used to lift a purely functional context to a social context.

171

Appendix

Match-making songs were popular. Here, the leader of the waulk-ing group, who always sung the line to lead off the choral response, matched a certain member of the group with a particular man in the village. The girl named then sung a reply. This dialogue was seldom truly spontaneous, as the address and the response had to fit in with certain traditional song forms and refrains, and indeed with the rhythm of the work. A typical instance was popular in Lewis. A refrain made up almost wholly of syllables was sung, with a fourth line bringing in a request for a sweetheart to be named. The lover suggested was then named in a single line sung by the soloist in the same melody as the one in which the request was made. If the man named was unacceptable, the response from the girl to whom the song was aimed was satrical:

Sios e sios e chuirt an uraich
'S a chuid luirichean ma cheann;
Ceigeanach dubh ceann gun chireadh
Cha teid mi gu dileann dha.
(Down with him, down with him to the dung yard with his rags of clothing, black dwarf of the unkempt head, I will never go to him.)

If the man was acceptable he would be eulogised:

Suas e suas e chuirt an airgid
Nighean a righ cha b'fharmad leam;
Suas e suas e bharr nan crannaibh
'S na siuil gheal' aic air a slinn.
(Up with him, up with him to the court of silver; I don't envy the daughter of the king; up he goes, up he goes to the tops of the masts, and her white sails heeling over.)

That many of the waulking songs, particularly their airs, are old, is evidenced by textual allusions to historical persons and events. Some date to the fifteenth century and earlier, to the times when the north-western seaboard of the Scottish mainland and its associated islands were a geographical, political and cultural unit with only tenuous connections with the seat of Scottish Government in Edinburgh.

In most waulking songs, poetic imagery is an outstanding feature. Most of this originates from acute observation of natural things and events which were real and accessible to the simple-living folk of the Highlands. Though the common people were often illiterate, the characteristic Celtic ability to create images was given expression. Imagery, in a highly developed form, occurs in many waulking songs, eg *Craobh nan Ubhal* (Apple Tree), (see page 178), and this imagery and the strength and beauty of their poetry, serves to underline, first, the creative characteristic of the Gael, and, secondly, the basic fidelity with which these themes come down into the twentieth century, their forms closely reflecting the original words. Though many stock phrases were used, as in the poetry of other languages, the results are often remarkable in their freshness.

In realising the finality of death : 'Sorrowful to me your curled hair being waulked in the seaweed; sorrowful to me your white teeth being torn asunder by the ocean'.

In a blessing for a sailor : 'In whichever harbour you may rest tonight, may there be merriment there and games and laughter, the striking of shoes and blisters upon palms, a frequent playing of chess and of the fair speckled cards'.

In a lament for a hunter : 'Alone on the sea-girt island and the birds remaining on the shore—well they may and forever; I have lost the hunter of the gun who would leave the brown deer on his knees and the grey seal from the wave-mouth'.

Though the stages at a waulking of course varied from two or three to anything up to twelve at a big waulking, the usual seven stages are generally distinguishable in the songs.

173

1 *Orain-teasachaidh* (heating-songs). These were fairly slow and gave the women time to get into the swing of the work.

2 *Orain-teannachaidh* (tightening-songs). These were lively and served to break the back of the work.

3 *Orain-shugraich* (frolic-songs). These were introduced to give the unmarried girls in the waulking party a chance to accept or reject an implied association with a sweetheart.

4 *Orain a' sineadh* (stretching-songs). The stretching was done to ensure the cloth was of even breadth.

5 *Orain a' baslachadh an aodaich* (clapping-songs). These accompanied the final light action to smooth the surface of the cloth.

6 *Coisrigheadh an aodaich* (consecration of the cloth). This was a kind of punctuation dedicating the work which had gone into the making of the cloth to the atttention of the Trinity, and invoking an assurance of the material's utility to the intended wearers.

7 *Orain a' coinnleachadh an aodaich* (folding-songs). These were used to accompany the ceremonial folding of the cloth before it was handed over to the owner.

THE CLIPPING BLESSING

Go shorn and come woolly,
Bear the Beltane female lamb,
Be the lovely Bride thee endowing,
And the fair Mary thee sustaining,
And the fair Mary sustaining thee.

SPINNING SONG

Cuigeal na Maighdin (The Distaff of the Maiden)

The distaff of the maiden, the distaff of the maiden,
A stocking on knitting pins, while sooty drops ooze from rafters.

Sleep littly baby, sleep little baby,
You did not spin the white cloth, you were asleep the
  night long.

THE CHANT OF THE WARPING

Thursday of beneficence,
For warping and waulking,
An hundred and fifty strands there shall be
  To number.

Blue thread, very fine,
Two of white by its side,
And scarlet by the side
  Of the madder.

My warp shall be very even,
Give to me Thy blessing, O God,
And to all who are beneath my roof
  In the dwelling.

Ward away every evil eye,
And all people of evil wishes,
Consecrate the woof and the warp
  Of every thread.

Place Thou Thine arm around
Each woman who shall be waulking it,
And do Thou aid her in the hour
  Of her need.

Since Thou, O God, it is who givest growth,
To each species and kind,
Give us wool from the surface
  Of the green grass.

Consecrate the flock in every place,
With their little lambs melodious, innocent,

And increase the generations
  Of our herds.

So that we may obtain from them wool,
And nourishing milk to drink,
And that no dearth may be ours
Of day clothing.

SUIDHEACHADH NA H-IOMAIRT

(Setting the Iomairt)

An dubh mu'n gheal,
An geal mu'n dubh,
An t-uain am meadhon an deirg,
An dearg am meadhon an duibh.

An dubh am meadhon an deirg,
An dearg am meadhon a ghil,
An geal am meadhon an uaine,
An t-uaine am meadhon a ghil.

An geal am meadhon a ghuirm,
An gorm am meadhon na sgarlaid.

An sgarlaid ris a ghorm,
An gorm ris an sgarlaid,
An sgarlaid ris an dubh,
An dubh ris an sgarlaid.

Snathla ri da shnathla
Do dha dhath,
Da shnathla dhubh,
Ri aon snathla geal.

Seachd snathla ri coig,
Coig ri tri,

Tri ri dha,
Dha ri aon,
Anns gach oir.

English version

The black by the white,
The white by the black,
The green in the middle of the red,
The red in the middle of the black.

The black in the middle of the red,
The red in the middle of the white,
The white in the middle of the green,
The green in the middle of the white.

The white in the middle of the blue,
The blue in the middle of the scarlet.

The scarlet to the blue,
The blue to the scarlet,
The scarlet to the black,
The black to the scarlet.

A thread to two threads
Of two colours,
Two threads of black,
To one thread of white.

Seven threads to five,
Five to three,
Three to two,
Two to one,
In each border.

Note: The *iomairt* is cloth striped lengthwise, not crosswise.
While the warp of the *iomairt* is composed of stripes of various

colours, the weft is confined to one, generally light blue, dark blue, or black. This cloth was confined to women's use. Setting the *iomairt*, like setting other warp, and setting eggs, was done on Thursday, that being the day of St Columba. Framing the web was a work of much anxiety to the housewife, and she and her maidens were up very early to put the thread in order. The thread of the *iomairt*, like that of the tartan, was very fine, hard-spun and double-twisted, rendering the cloth extremely durable.

CRAOBH NAN UBHAL

(The Apple Tree)

O apple tree,
Apple branch,
Apple tree,
   Tree of apples.

When thou goest to the wood to strip it,
Recognise the tree which is mine there,
The tree of softest, sweetest apples,
The branching pear-like tree full of apples,
Its roots growing and its top bending.

I have a tree in the Green Rock,
Another tree hard by the garden gate;
If MacKay were but here,
Or the redoubtable Neil, his brother,
My dower would not go unpaid,
With milch kine and heifers in calf,
With sheep black-faced and white,
And with geldings for the ploughing.

A versatile man is MacKay,
He can make silk of May wool,
And satin of heather if need were,
He can make wine of mountain water.

An ingenious man is MacKay,
He can dry grain without fuel,
It is with his fists he bruises it.

MacKay of the gusseted coat
Would not require heavy armour,
Rider of the chestnut horses,
He would put golden shoes on their hooves,
Traverser of the broken ground.

O apple tree, may God be with thee,
May the moon and the sun be with thee,
May the east and west winds be with thee,
May everything that ever existed be with thee,
May every bounty and desire be with thee,
May every passion and divinity be with thee,
May great Somerled and his band be with thee,
May everyone, like myself, be with thee.

ORAN LUAIDH IORTACH
(A St Kilda Waulking Song)

Hill hu hill ho
Hill ho ro bha ho
Hill hu hill ho
Thou wouldst be my support didst thou come.

I should prefer to all the cattle I have got
To be in St Kilda plucking the guillemots,
Hill hu ho.

Along with the grey-billed solan goose
Which snatches the fish from the surface of the current.
Hill hu ho.

Thou youth with the top-boots,
Thou wilt go to the byre before I can sit down.
Hill hu ho.

179

Thou wouldst dance strongly and vigorously,
Without ever bending thy knees.
Hill hu ho.

Thou wilt bring the fulmar and the garefowl,
And the cormorant from the point of the cape.
Hill hu ho.

Thou wilt go to the great mainland of Kintail
Along with tall Ivar of the Brae.
Hill hu hill ho.

ORAN CUARTACHAIDH
(Circuiting Song)

Hill! hill! ho! Hillin O!
Hill! is ho ro bha o!

Last night I got not a wink of sleep,
Hill hill! ho! hillin o!
This night I shall not get as much,
Hill! hill! ho! hillin o!

Though she were tattered and shaggy,
Fat and fair are her father's cattle.

Though she were wizened and shrivelled,
Fair and white are her horned cattle.

Though she were hungry and like death,
Oh my love the hidden windfall!

Though her eyes were watery, hollow,
And her mouth like amber, she'll get a lover.

But I lie snug, easy and sleepful,
Without cattle black or red or dappled.

Last night I got not a wink of sleep,
    Hill! hill! ho! hillin o!
This night I shall not get as much,
    Hill! hill! ho! hillin o!

Note: This song was sung by girls going round the waulking frame. Each girl was given the opportunity to try her talent at impromptu verse and they bantered each other about their lovers, or supposed lovers. The above song was by a girl whose lover left her for another endowed with more worldly goods.

BASRADH
(Hand-smoothing)

Mayest thou wear the cloth
    To shreds,
Mayest thou wear the cloth
    To rags,
Mayest thou wear the cloth
With food and music
In every way
    As we would fain have thee;

     In thy modesty,
     In thy health,
     In thy friends,
      In thy love,
     In the grace of the Father,
     In the grace of the Son,
     In the grace of the Spirit,
      In the grace of the Three of the elements.

Note: When the cloth was being piled up, the waulking women smoothed it out with their palms and blessed it: 'To the Father, To the Son, To the Spirit'. Then before the waulking party left

the house, the mother of sons went up to the man of the house
and said the above verses to him.

COISRIGEADH AN AODAICH
(Consecration of the cloth)

FIRST CONSECRATOR:
>   I give the sunwise turn
>   Dependent on the Father.

SECOND CONSECRATOR:
>   I give the sunwise turn
>   Dependent on the Son.

THIRD CONSECRATOR:
>   I give the sunwise turn
>   Dependent on the Spirit.

THE THREE CONSECRATORS:
>   And each sunwise turn
>   Dependent on the Three,
>   And each turn it takes
>   For the sake of the THREE

>   And each sunwise turn
>   Dependent on the Three.

BEANNACHADH
(Blessing)

>   This is no second-hand cloth,
>   And it is not begged,
>   It is not property of cleric,
>   It is not property of priest,
>   And it is not property of pilgrim;

But thine own property,
O son of my body,
By moon and by sun,
In the presence of God,
And keep thou it!

Mayest thou enjoy it,
Mayest thou wear it,
Mayest thou finish it,
Until thou find it
In shreds,
In strips,
In rags,
In tatters!

THE MUSIC OF WAULKING-SONGS

Discounting Gaelic music composed formally over the past century or so, and which tends to conform to the more conventional eight-note scale, virtually all Gaelic folk music is based on the pentatonic scale, with five notes (C to C^1 with the third and seventh degrees omitted). Within this basic scale there are five positions or groupings of notes to give the modes which are known as Ionian, Lydian (rare in Gaelic), Dorian, Aeolian, and Phrygian (rare in Gaelic). In these pentatonic scales the determination of the tonic or commencing note is much more doubtful than in the scales to which modern ears are accustomed. However, many Gaelic tunes are based on a true hexatonic scale. The minor character is common in Gaelic folk-music, though the major often appears; major and minor to suggest mood in music is largely ignored and rather more emphasis is placed on the text of the song. Gaelic music is noted for its characteristic use of non-essential or grace-notes, which are sharpened or flattened to give the basic tune a distinctive flavour.

The modal character of Gaelic music is not peculiar to the

Scottish Highlands. It occurs in the folk music of other countries and is therefore a stamp of antiquity. As Sir Hubert Parry says: 'Nearly all the pentatonic scales have been filled in, and the nations who use them are familiar with other notes besides the curious and characteristic formula of five; but in the background of their musical feeling the original foundation of their system remains distinct'.

Gaelic folk-music shows a distinct liking for five-beat and seven-beat rhythms; in this respect it is similar to Scandinavian folk music. Combinations of rhythms are also found, such as five to the bar, followed by three to the bar. The system of accents in a language influences its poetry and music, for it determines the rhythm. In Gaelic, the accent or beat is most often on the first syllable of the word. For this reason, there are few poems or songs in Gaelic ending on a strong accent; while the reverse is true of English ones. The usual rule in Gaelic is that the line should end in a strong accent followed by a secondary or weak accent. In folk-song, remarkable peculiarities are to be found in the cadences. One reason for this is that many songs were labour songs which required continuity and were therefore 'circular' in character; they ended on their weakest part or on an incomplete end. Though occasionally a particular modal conception has caused a weak cadence, the reason is more often to be attributed to the peculiarities in the language. In this respect, it is interesting that weak endings are not nearly so common in Irish Gaelic, though the roots of both Scots and Irish Gaelic are the same. This is because the system of Irish accents is different and requires a strong finish to a line or musical phrase.

Gaelic tunes are all characterised by a good balance between harmonic and melodic expression, by order and symmetry, in spite of the great variety of song structures that exist. In addition, there is a characteristic soft and quite beautiful musical form. The songs, many from functional derivations, all bear witness to the high standard and sense of music in the people who created them and it is sad to admit that the present day is witnessing their decay. With the introduction of alien cultural and material influences there has been a tendency to forget many of the important aspects which made Gaelic culture something able to stand on its own inherent strength in line with the cultures of other countries. Much has been preserved on paper and on tape, but the days when a song collector could go to a singer in the Hebrides and record from her 345 songs in twelve days, as well as a number of tales and interesting snippets of information about past customs and beliefs, are fast disappearing, and with them perhaps the essential elements which gave the Hebrides and, in former times at least, the western seaboard of Gaelic Scotland, distinct and socially-significant ideas of community living.

Index

The numbers in italics refer to plates and illustrations in text

introduction to Highlands 31; Scottish Blackface *18*, 30, 79, 137; Tan-faced 30; White-faced 30
'Shepherd's Check', 19
Shielabost, *35*
shuttle, 45, 46; flying, 73
Simon, Lord, 118
Sinclair, Sir John, 31
Skye, 47, 48, 60
Small, Susan, 153
Smith, Lewis, 128
Smith, Roderick, 70
Smith & Company (Stornoway), Thomas, 116, 119, 128
South Uist, 60, 85, 109, 124, 131
Spectator, 152
'Spanish Champagne' case, 133
spindle, 41 et seq, *41*, *43*, 139
spinning; hand 40, *42*, 43, *43*, 80, 125, *144*; mill 73, 93, 139; mule 139; song 174; whorls, 28, 29, 41, *41*, see also Harris Tweed
stake-warping, *36*
stamping (Orb mark), 87, *89*, *98*, 105, *123*, 140
stannous chloride, 33
St Kilda: 23, 50 et seq, 87, 109; loom *107*; *waulking song* 179
Stornoway: 14, 23, 81, *90*, 124, 148; Tweed 74
Stornoway Gazette, 112, 113
'Stornoway' take-up motion, 142
stretching tweed, *143*
Sutherland, Harriet Duchess of, 59, 62, 76, 102
Sutherland Home Industries, 62
synthetic dyes, 79

Tan-faced sheep, see sheep
Tarbert, 14, 70, 80, 81, 105, 148
temperature, 16
Thomas, Mrs F. W., 59
tin, 33
Tolmie, Frances, 48
Tolmie & Co Ltd, D., 128
Trade Marks Act, 77, 101
Transport & General Workers Union, 116, 145
truck system, 64
Tuffin, Marion, 153

Tweed: description 24-5; output *92*, *122*, *129*; setting-up 54; Stornoway 74; tying-in *53*; weave 24; see also Harris Tweed and Lewis Tweed
twill, 24-5
'two and two' twill, 24

Uig, 70, 81, 148
United Kingdom market, 138
USA market, 138
upholstery, 153
urine, 33, 51, 55

vegetable dyes, 79

War Office, 91
warp, 44; mill-spun 75
warping, 44; chant 175; process, *36*, 44, 80, 139
washing, *72*
Watsons of Hawick, 26
waulking, 46 et seq; in Barra 50; in Benbecula 50; in Faroes 55; in Finland 55; in Hebrides 47; in Iceland 55; in Norway 55; in Orkney 52; present-day 151; in St Kilda 50; in Skye 47-8; songs 170 et seq; stages 46, 173; in Sweden 55; woman in Harris *143*; women in Lewis *126*
weaver, *53*, *54*, 71,*126*, 144
weaving: ancient 28; combs 28, *29*; as an economic activity 19, 140; loom (Hattersley) *54*; loom (wooden beam), *126*, *144*; process 44, 80, 139
weft, 44; hand-spun 75
West Riding of Yorkshire, 26
White-faced sheep, see sheep
wind, 16
woad, 32
Wool, see under processes eg clipping or scouring, sheep, Harris Tweed
Wool clip, 79, 119, 137
worsted cloth, 139

yarn: 42, 45, 82; island mill-spun 95; mainland mill-spun 95

Zelker, Sybil, 153